Look What God Has Done:

the First 20 Years

Look What God Has Done:

the First 20 Years

Edd McGrath & Holly Ogden

Christian Motorcyclists Association, Inc.
PO Box 9
Hatfield, AR 71945
www.cmausa.org

Copyright © 2007 by Christian Motorcyclists Association, Inc.

Cover art designed by Meri Brock.

Unless otherwise noted, Scripture quotations are taken from the *Holy Bible*, New International Version ®. NIV®. Copyright © 1973, 1978, 1984 by International Bible Society. Used by permission. All rights reserved.

The "NIV" and "New International Version" trademarks are registered in the United States Patent and Trademark Office by International Bible Society. Use of either trademark requires the permission of International Bible Society.

Scripture quotations marked NLT are taken from the *Holy Bible*, New Living Translation, copyright 1996. Used by permission of Tyndale House Publishers, Inc., Wheaton, Illinois 60189. All rights reserved.

Scripture quotations marked NKJV™ are from the *Holy Bible*, New King James Version®. Copyright © 1979, 1980, 1982 by Thomas Nelson, Inc. Used by permission. All rights reserved.

ISBN 978-1-60402-108-0

Printed in the United States of America.

We dedicate this book to the members of the Christian Motorcyclists Association for their perseverance in *changing the world, one heart at a time.*

Table of Contents

SECTION FOUR: HOMELAND MISSIONS

SECTION FIVE: FOREIGN MISSIONS

SECTION SIX: CONCLUSION

Definitions of Abbreviations

Christian Motorcyclists Association   CMA

Run for the Son   RFS

Missionary Ventures International   MVI

Open Doors   OD

The JESUS Film Project   JFP

Preface

In celebration of the 20th anniversary of Run for the Son, members of the Christian Motorcyclists Association will tell you how CMA and RFS have changed their lives. Over and over you will hear them say, "My life was changed forever." As we reviewed each story, we preserved the "voice" of the writer so that you can hear the rich texture of the big and diverse community that is the Christian Motorcyclists Association. Some of the letters will make you laugh; some will make you cry. But we hope all of them will move you out of your comfort zone as you continue your walk with the Lord.

So we present to you the many voices of CMA. May you be blessed as you read!

Edd McGrath, Co-Editor

Acknowledgements

We would like to thank the Spirit of God for making such a book as this a possibility. Without Him, and His inspiration to begin the Run for the Son 20 years ago, countless lives would have remained untouched by the love of Jesus Christ. He has guided us as we have gathered the testimonies from members throughout the nation so that we may proclaim His love to the world.

We would also like to thank the many people who have participated in the Run for the Son, both those recorded in this book and those not recorded.

We would like to extend a special thanks to Edd McGrath, Holly Ogden, Mary Kelley, Missy Parmenter, Wendy McDaniel, and the rest of the team who helped us to compile the book and for all the time and energy they have invested into this project.

SECTION ONE:
Ministry Partners' Reflections

Changing the World, One Heart at a Time

John Ogden, CEO/Chairman of the Board of Directors, Christian Motorcyclists Association, CMA No. 7,757

CMA's vision is to *change the world, one heart at a time* with a strong belief in the biblical principle of giving. We have looked for ways to touch the heart of God, through outreach to bikers and other ministries with world-reaching potential.

When God planted the thought and the plans for RFS in the minds of man, it opened a door that enabled us to extend our heart throughout the world. Through this fundraising effort we have been blessed with the opportunity to give 60% of the funds raised each year to three partners in ministry: Missionary Ventures International, Open Doors, and The JESUS Film Project. Over the course of the RFS, there has been over $24 million raised to fund ministry within the United States and throughout the world. Through this,

- 7.2 million+ people have come to know Jesus Christ.
- 1.3 million Bibles have been sent to closed countries.
- 2,600 motorcycles have been given to indigenous pastors in over 95 countries.
- 39 million people have seen the *JESUS* film.

Closer to home, RFS has allowed CMA to be more effective in taking the gospel of Jesus Christ to bikers throughout the United States, as proceeds have made it possible for us to develop outreach ministry tools in the form of tracts, training material, and servant ministries. It has enabled us to develop leadership training material and hold leadership conferences to equip Christian leaders to build a foundation for CMA members involved in ministry to bikers. It has also permitted us to keep a team of Evangelists spread throughout the United States training and developing people for the work of the ministry, as well as presenting the gospel of Jesus to bikers. Our members have been able to touch untold lives and hearts, made possible through RFS.

Christian Motorcyclists Association Impact

Steve Beam, President, Missionary Ventures International, CMA No. 29,741

2007 marks the 20th anniversary of the partnership that Missionary Ventures International, or MVI, shares with CMA. It has been one of the most fantastic and wonderful partnerships that MVI has enjoyed in missions.

When Edd McGrath, a CMA member and an MVI Board member, introduced CMA to our Board, we all laughed. It seemed, at the time, an oxymoron. "A **CHRISTIAN** motorcycle group?" we all exclaimed.

Edd explained that he had called the leadership of CMA to tell them about a *problem* we were having in trying to supply pastors and evangelists with motorcycles so they could go to remote areas in Guatemala. CMA said they were willing to help and would sponsor a fundraising campaign called *Run for the Son*. They hoped to be able to help a few pastors with bikes.

But the MVI Board was still very cautious, and felt unanimous about sending Edd (by himself) to the CMA rally in Arizona to receive the RFS proceeds. When Edd returned, he dropped a check for $40,000 on the table to buy motorcycles for the Guatemalan pastors. He then announced that we were going to Guatemala to host a delegation from CMA to give away the bikes. A few months later, I stood on the balcony of the Guatemala City Airport waiting for some bikers to come through the gates, not knowing who or what to expect.

When I spotted them, they looked like the typical bikers who would cause me to lock my doors if they rode by my car— but they acted differently. They knelt in the dirt to pray, they shared their testimonies of God's grace in their lives, and they generously gave and wept when each of the 21 motorcycles were handed over to the Guatemalan pastors. God touched

2

their lives and ours that very day, and as a result, our hearts have been knit together ever since.

From that first RFS campaign to this day, God has been using CMA in some incredible ways in missions in North America and throughout the globe. They have given over 2,600 motorcycles and 4,200 bicycles to indigenous pastors and evangelists in 95 countries.

Thousands of churches have been planted in unreached areas, countless lives have been touched on mission trips, and millions of miles have been covered on paths, roads, and byways that have never been reached with the gospel.

Through our partnership, I have learned about *real* missions and outreach and why God is blessing CMA so abundantly. I know few Christian groups, churches, or denominations that report this kind of force and mission. CMA is doing it because:

- The majority of time, talent, funds, and energy go into winning souls for Jesus.
- There isn't a dress code, church style code, or good behavior code to become a Christian. In fact, people are reached that would not darken the door of a church; but, more importantly, the very people against whom most of us would lock our doors if we passed them on *our* way to church.
- Christ is the center of teaching and the reason for fellowship and mission.
- Anyone can be used as part of the process. Yes, there are a handful of "professional" CMA evangelists, but their main job is to equip and encourage the thousands who are really out among the multitude of bikers, clubs, and gangs, winning them to Christ.
- There is not one superstar man or woman upon whom all eyes focus. Yes, the leadership could run any Fortune 500 company, but the objective is not to see how great any*one* is. Rather it is to proclaim the gospel through as many bikers around the globe as possible.

One of my most profound experiences witnessing the impact of these motorcycles carrying Christian workers "where no one has gone before," was in the heart of the jungle in Peru. Our party had traveled for days through the deep Amazon jungle to reach our destination. It was a small village of Ketchwah Indians, cut off and hidden from the outside world and living as they did 300 years ago. As we walked into the adobe church building with a dirt floor and thatched roof, I quietly wondered: How in the world did this village get discovered, who found these people, and how in the world did they get here to start this outreach? My thoughts were interrupted by the sound of a muffler echoing its thunderous applause, announcing its entrance into the village. I turned to see a Peruvian pastor riding up on his CMA motorcycle. There was my answer!

What would Jesus ride if He lived in human flesh today? I don't know what bike He'd prefer, but I do know He'd be on the road reaching out to those in the greatest need of His love, healing, and forgiveness. He'd also be calling ordinary people to follow Him and do the same, just like the Christian Motorcyclists Association.

Open Doors

Carl Moeller, President/CEO, Open Doors, USA, CMA No. 120,131

I wanted to take a few moments to share with you the impact that RFS has had on our work. Your faithfulness, boldness, and enthusiasm in doing this unique event for 20 years have made our partnership like family.

I remember the first time I heard the words, "Run for the Son." I was the brand-new president of Open Doors, USA and did not yet realize the amazing relationship we had with CMA. My heart was encouraged as I found out more—that CMA and Open Doors had provided millions of Bibles through RFS. I called John Ogden and introduced myself; his encouragement was a positive introduction to our long-standing relationship.

A couple of years later as John and I were in a Muslim country we saw the power of bikers assembled together for Christ. We witnessed the very first "Christian biker rally" in that country. They displayed the power of God to encourage and mobilize believers as they used their motorcycles as witnessing and ministry tools. John spoke to the hearts of these bikers—men who daily face persecution because of their Christian witness in that country.

CMA—you are much like the evangelists in that country... You are stepping out in faith, boldly proclaiming Christ, and making a real difference in places where others will not go. That is why I feel that we are "family."

Family traits are obvious when you look at the physical—like a big nose or big ears or flat feet—but they are also clear when we look at the spiritual dimensions of our lives. Our brothers and sisters in Christ are recognizable—I see them in the places where "faith costs the most;" but I also see the same characteristics in you, CMA. Your perseverance, your zeal, your generosity, your passion for Jesus, all feels familiar—you are family!

RFS has been the vehicle that has brought our common mission together. God has used RFS to unleash kingdom resources like never before. Your support of persecuted Christians has enabled Open Doors co-workers to bring God's Word to millions of believers in China, India, Colombia, Indonesia, and over 45 other countries, it has helped provide literacy training and pastoral training in many of these countries, and it has enabled us to be a "voice for the voiceless" in America and the free world.

Congratulations to CMA for 20 years of RFS–blessings to all of your members who have committed to making this extraordinary event happen–and ALL GLORY TO GOD for HIS abundant provision. Thank YOU!

Reaching the World for Christ through Partnerships

Chris McQuirk, Red River Regional Manager, The JESUS Film Project, CMA No. 67,834

When I think about the impact CMA and RFS has had on worldwide evangelization, I think of words like global, life changing, strategic, eternal, momentous, far-reaching, and radical.

In 1997, CMA gave the first gift to The JESUS Film Project, a $10,000 donation. We never asked for that original gift. CMA gave it as part of their "tithe." When I called to thank CMA, I received an invitation from their president (Herbie Shreve) to attend the next rally in Hatfield, Arkansas. At that time, I knew almost nothing about the ministry of CMA–I didn't even know where Hatfield was! I told Herbie that I would check my schedule and get back with him. It didn't take me long to realize, after looking at a map, that Hatfield was situated right in the "middle of nowhere."

I decided to make the trip to Hatfield in October 1997. Herbie asked me to give a presentation about The JESUS Film Project. At the end of my presentation (which included a short video), Herbie announced the CMA Board of Directors had decided to add The JEUS Film Project as one of their RFS ministry partners. He looked at me and asked how I would feel if they were able to give $200,000 the next year. Of course I was excited and a little shocked. I never thought this first trip to Hatfield would begin a relationship and partnership that has lasted nearly a decade.

Gifts from CMA (1997 to 2006) have totaled $3,969,971. These funds have been used to:

- Support teams all over the world showing the *JESUS* film.
- Provide equipment used to show the film (projectors, screens, generators, etc.).
- Provide transportation for teams showing the film.

- Provide follow-up literature.
- Provide training for rural church planters.
- Provide new lip-sync translations of the *JESUS* film.

CMA has made a huge impact on the world through the RFS, touching numerous countries like: India, Sri Lanka, Nepal, Bhutan, Turkey, Togo, Ethiopia, Swaziland, Zimbabwe, Zambia, Uganda, Kenya, Djibouti, Botswana, Algeria, Afghanistan, Lesotho, Madagascar, Mozambique, Namibia, South Africa, Tanzania, China, Malawi, Congo, Sudan, Palestine, Lebanon, Egypt, Syria, Armenia, Pakistan, Slovenia, Thailand, Viet Nam, Russia, Philippines, Laos, Cambodia, Nigeria, and Colombia, just to name a few!

Historically, [1]an average of 10 people worldwide will see the *JESUS* film and one will make a decision to follow Christ for every dollar donated. If this average holds true for CMA's donations, then CMA has been able to expose over 39 million people to the gospel and 3.9 million have made decisions for Christ.

In addition to the incredible impact CMA has had on reaching out to some of the most difficult areas of the world, it is also exciting to watch and help cultivate the growing partnerships between CMA, The JESUS Film Project, Missionary Ventures International, and Open Doors. In 2005, all four ministries planned a "team-building" ministry trip together, which has since become an annual event, with the payer that we will accomplish something for the Lord together that our individual ministries could not do alone.

Headed for Colombia in September 2006, I was responsible for organizing a cooperative showing of the *JESUS* film with three ministries that had never formally worked together! What follows is an overview of that trip.

---

[1] As The JESUS Film Project continues to reach the neglected people of the world, this figure may change.

MAY 2006: FIRST TRIP—UNPLANNED!

As I was planning the team-building trip, CMA asked me to take part in a separate short-term mission trip. Although I had misgivings, I began making plans. The enemy, however, was working overtime in his attempt to thwart this trip, causing one problem after another. This attack confirmed I was to participate in both trips.

My goal was to try to connect the Colombian staff of The JESUS Film Project, or JFP, Missionary Ventures, and Open Doors. Missionary Ventures missionary, Billy Castro, presented us with a unique opportunity to show the *JESUS* film on the largest military base in Colombia. It was Billy's non-Christian uncle (a general) who granted this permission. Wow...what an opportunity!

We were able to show *JESUS* to about 600 soldiers, 160 committed their lives to Christ! After the film, we passed out more than 600 Spanish Bibles donated by Open Doors.

Before we left, the base commander extended an open-ended invitation to return anytime and show the film again! I thought, 'What an incredible open door.' Together we CAN accomplish more!

SEPTEMBER 2006—A NEW PLAN

Before leaving for the actual trip, leaders of three of our four ministries met to plan ways for their respective field staff to maximize the openness that now existed within the Colombian military for sharing the gospel through the *JESUS* film. It was after this meeting that Wilson Moreno (JFP), Miguel Perez (Open Doors), and Billy Castro (MV) shared the following:

> *We see this team as a powerful model for the body of Christ here in Colombia, demonstrating that age-old walls preventing the body from functioning in a healthy way can be toppled IF we allow the Spirit of God to lead, AND employ good stewardship in using our gifts and talents to advance HIS kingdom.*

9

THE RESULTS—AND THE FUTURE!

Over the following 12 months, Colombian soldiers going through boot camp saw the *JESUS* film and participated in 2½ days of basic Christian follow-up training. Four such weekend seminars took place at the same base where we first showed the film. The plan, *The Army Boot Camp Outreach,* had the potential to reach 1,000 soldiers each presentation. The newly formed partnership used the *JESUS* film as the key evangelistic tool in reaching young military recruits. This would have never happened had it not been for CMA and RFS.

ETERNAL TREASURES FOR GOD'S KINGDOM!

CMA has many important aspects of ministry, but the ministry of giving is making an eternal impact far beyond what our minds can comprehend. The bikers of CMA, who give their time and talents to make RFS a success, are laying up treasures in heaven–treasures that will last for all eternity.

Thank you, CMA for your partnership with us! Together we really are changing the world, one heart at a time!

SECTION TWO:

The Early Days

In the Beginning

Edd McGrath, Missionary Ventures International Board of Directors, CMA No. 20,193

Run for the Son began for me in 1953 when I was thirteen years old. I am amazed at the picture the Lord weaves in the tapestry of my life as He adds one thread to another. Like most Christians, I usually don't recognize the importance of each single thread as it is added to the picture. One of those threads was red–a little red Harley I bought in 1953 with money I had earned in the cornfields of Illinois. It offered freedom, and was the birth of my motorcycle life.

By 1985, I had lived in Florida for twenty-two years, and was riding a BMW to escape the pressures of a white-collar life. I was a real estate professional, but I spent a lot of time in ministry with my church and various para-church organizations. I was a subscriber to *Road Rider* magazine (years later, it morphed into *Motorcycle Consumer News*). *Road Rider* listed ride meets, which included information about Christians having breakfast together. I thought, 'Wow! It would be great to ride to breakfast and meet other Christian bikers.' One of the articles in *Road Rider* mentioned an organization that I had never heard of–CMA. Interesting. I glanced through the classified ads and found a small ad encouraging people interested in joining CMA to write to Herb Shreve in Hatfield, Arkansas. Not wanting to take the time to write, I decided to call Herb (Hatfield was a small place; I figured that I should be able to locate him). Sure enough, I found his number and called him. His wife, Shirley, answered the call, but I couldn't speak with Herb because he was recovering from a heart problem. Shirley took my name and number and said someone would get in touch with me.

For several weeks I heard nothing. Then one day I received a call from Sherman Davis, a member of the Royal Riders CMA chapter in Bartow, Florida, about sixty miles from where I lived. Sherman said they were having a breakfast meeting the following Saturday and I was welcome to join them. I told him I'd be there. I rode to the meeting, enjoyed the fellowship, and soon joined CMA and the Royal Riders chapter. I got my CMA card shortly thereafter.

I joined CMA to enjoy the fellowship of other Christian motorcyclists and to ride with them. I wasn't looking for ministry; I was looking to escape the pressures of a lot of other ministries and responsibilities I already had. Royal Riders was a former church riding group that had become a CMA chapter and it suited my purpose very well.

One of the ministry groups I was involved with was MVI. In the fall of 1987, I was in Guatemala with the rest of the MVI Board of Directors. We were on a five-day trip to inspect some of our outreach efforts there. On the last day before we were to fly back to Florida, we met with Missionary Paul Diltz in his home. One of the MVI Board members made a joke about my being a biker. (In those days a man who spent his work days in a three-piece suit and also rode a motorcycle was uncommon.) Paul never picked up on the joke, but he immediately picked up on the word *motorcycle*. He pulled out a picture of a Guatemalan pastor seated on a used, dual-purpose motorcycle. Paul said that small motorcycles, like the one in the picture, were a great aid in helping native pastors spread the gospel. He then turned to me and asked if I would raise some money to buy more motorcycles. I told him I would.

As I left the airport the next morning to fly back to Tampa I thought about the commitment I had made to Paul and realized I had no idea how to raise money for motorcycles. I thought, 'If nothing else, I can just buy him a motorcycle or two.'

I got back to my Florida office on Tuesday and on Friday, I left for a weekend CMA campout in Lake Wales, a small town about sixty-five miles east of Tampa. When my riding buddy, Bob Joliffe, and I arrived at the campground, I was still thinking about my trip to Guatemala and the promise I made to Paul Diltz.

Around the campfire that night guys were talking about their motorcycles and the new chrome they had bought and I was thinking about what that money could do on the mission field. Also attending that very casual rally was Herbie Shreve [who would later become President of CMA], son of CMA Founder, Herb Shreve. I had met Herbie at the Seasons of Refreshing and CMA Florida State Rally and enjoyed his fellowship during my then three years in CMA, so I approached him with an idea. I told Herbie of my need for money for motorcycles. He got excited about CMA becoming involved in foreign missions and asked me to send him information on MVI.

That presented a problem. CMA had all of those neat t-shirts, stickers, a national newspaper, and several hundred chapters scattered around the United States, Canada, and a few other places. MVI, on the other hand, was a bare-bones six-year-old upstart. We were strong on field work, but short on slick promotional materials. I gathered up every little brochure and scrap of paper that MVI had and sent it to Herbie. In January 1988, I had another interview with him and Southeast Regional Evangelist, Tom Pittman, at the CMA Florida Seasons of Refreshing in Ocala. I again gave them my pitch and more bits of MVI information. They said they would get back to me.

I didn't hear anything during February, and I was beginning to think CMA had forgotten me. Then one morning Herbie called. He said that while riding through Texas the Lord showed him that CMA should have a one-day national fund-raiser. He said they would call it Run for the Son and he promised to give MVI 20% of the amount CMA raised.

The first RFS was on Saturday, May 7, 1988. We turned in our collected donations and called in the total to the CMA headquarters in Hatfield. By the first of the next week, we realized we had made our national goal of $200,000.

The 1988 CMA National Rally was in Williams, Arizona, on the south rim of the Grand Canyon. Janet and I flew from Tampa, FL to Flagstaff, AZ, where we rented a nearly new

Yamaha Venture. We loaded our gear on the Yamaha and headed to the rally. When the RFS money was awarded we picked up a $40,000 check for MVI. CMA also gave a check for $80,000 to Open Doors that year. The men who received the check looked like IBM salesmen, dressed in white shirts, ties, and dark suits. One of those guys was Bob Hawley, then the administrative head of Open Doors. Bob, who became a good friend, later told me they left their wives and kids at a motel because they didn't know what to expect from this group of bikers.

Janet and I flew back to Tampa and gave the $40,000 check to the MVI Board. There had been a few skeptics among the board members, but that check made believers out of all of them.

In October 1988, Janet and I headed to Central America with seven other CMAers to begin giving away the 21 motorcycles we had purchased with the RFS money. We gave seven motorcycles to pastors with whom Paul Diltz was working. The pastors and their families had prepared a feast for us to say 'thank you' for the bikes. We were so humbled by their gift that we could hardly eat.

There were two men who went with that group to Central America who stand out in my memory. One was Richard Grill, a former CMA Area Rep from Pennsylvania. Richard looked like the kind of guy you wouldn't want to meet in a dark alley. He had a shaved head, a full beard, a muscular body, and heavy boots–an intimidating figure! Yet, when we gave away a motorcycle and he spoke, he started to cry. This big, tough guy had a soft heart for the Lord and for the people. Richard continued to go to Central America for several years to minister to those he had met on that first trip.

The other fellow was a chap from Canada. He was skeptical about our collecting money to buy motorcycles. He had come on this trip to see if we would really do what we said we were going to do, and he saw that we were true to our word. That first mission trip changed his life.

16

Over and over on this first CMA mission trip, pastors who received the bikes told us they had prayed for a bike for a year or two before we began RFS. The Lord made it plain that this was not our idea, but His. As the Scripture says, it is not he who plants or he who waters, but God who gives the increase.

CAN WE DO IT AGAIN?

The 1988 RFS was the first national fundraiser CMA had undertaken. It worked out well, we met our financial goal, and we had seen the fruit of our efforts in the third-world. Not all was well though—the national economy was falling into recession beginning in the fourth quarter of 1988 and things were not looking good.

In 1989, in the midst of a national recession, the RFS goal was increased and we met the goal. We *could* do it again! The following year, the RFS goal was increased, and again CMA came through and met the goal. It was plain that God was blessing our efforts and showing He could provide, regardless of the national economy. Each year the goal was increased, and each year we met the goal. During the 1993 CMA National Rally in Sedalia, Missouri, there was a feeling that CMA had really bought into RFS. It was no longer a question about whether we could do it; the RFS had become an important part of the life of CMA.

We were also seeing the fruit of taking CMA members to the mission field. Early on, mission trips were given to those who were leaders in the RFS fundraising efforts. In MVI, we had long had an emphasis on the impact of the mission experience on the spiritual life of those who took the trips. To MVI the supplying of resources to the third-world church was only part of the picture—the rest of the picture was what was happening in the hearts of the people who went on those trips. We wanted to get our United States brethren out of their comfort zone and let them see the rest of the world.

We were up and running—for the SON!

Open Doors

Brother Andrew, Founder Open Doors International

I have said many times that our mission is called *Open Doors* because we believe any door is open, anytime, anywhere...to proclaim Christ (Revelation 3:8). Open Doors' partnership with CMA and RFS through the years has enabled Open Doors to do just that—open doors previously closed by bringing the gospel around the world.

The faithfulness and generosity of CMA through RFS has impacted our ministry and, in turn, our suffering brothers and sisters in Christ. In 2005 alone, Open Doors delivered 5.4 million Bibles, children's Bibles, study Bibles, and other scriptural books and literature to persecuted Christians. Also, Open Doors trained 107,000 Christian leaders.

I have met with believers in such places as China and the Islamic world who had tears in their eyes after being presented with the precious Word of God. CMA stood alongside Open Doors field workers and the persecuted church with their support and prayers.

I consider CMA not only blessed partners, but wonderful friends. What a pleasure it was to go to CMA headquarters in 2005 to celebrate CMA's 30th anniversary. It was also a time to celebrate thirty years of being faithful to its mission of taking the gospel of Jesus Christ to not only bikers, but to the entire world.

Congratulations on twenty years of sponsoring the RFS. The results have been life-changing and heart-changing. On behalf of Open Doors and members of the persecuted church, thank you. May the Lord continue to bless the Run for the Son and your ministry!

Christian Bikers?

Bob Hawley, Formerly Open Doors, CMA No. 36,796

It was late spring of 1988 when my office received a call from a representative of CMA. He asked if someone from Open Doors with Brother Andrew could come to a rally they were having in Williams, Arizona. The explanation was that CMA had completed a fundraiser and wished to give a gift to the Open Doors ministry.

I called our regional representative and asked if he would like to travel to the south rim of the Grand Canyon to meet with this group. He was reluctant. One of the light-hearted comments was, "This group is a biker gang and they're looking for some Christian to sacrifice at the Grand Canyon." Other comments were really in the form of questions: "Are there Christians who ride motorcycles?" and "Do you really believe there is a biker group by that name?"

I told our staff that I would be willing to make the trip to visit with these people. They promised to pray for my trip (and for my safe return). I responded, "If we can send people into Communist lands to deliver Bibles, we should be able to face whatever dangers God takes us through here."

When I arrived at the campsite in Williams, Arizona in the early afternoon, I was greeted warmly by Herb Shreve and his son, Herbie. They invited me to sit at a nearby picnic table to visit. The conversation went directly to how they were introduced to Brother Andrew by reading his book, *God's Smuggler*. They were intrigued that one man would be willing to enter a country going through internal revolution to take Bibles to the Christians. I explained communism was a religion and their religion didn't allow for any other religions. Christianity was a direct challenge to what they wanted to do in each country they controlled. As they entered a country, they would confiscate every piece of literature that taught a belief in God. As atheists, there was no room in their religion for faith in God.

Every Bible, every hymnbook, and every piece of Christian literature was to be burned.

Brother Andrew understood their system of attack and he knew the church needed the living Word of God. Out of obedience to God's call, he drove his Volkswagen into every country he could. Many times the Christians told him that his being there was worth ten of the best sermons they had ever heard. Andrew knew preaching was not his calling, but giving encouragement was something anyone could do, so he went.

Herb and Herbie told me they had attended a fundraising banquet sponsored by Open Doors and learned of the desperate need for Bibles. They went home with that thought heavy on their hearts.

I told them a little about my background as a pastor and trips overseas to visit with Christians. I invited them to travel with me someday to see, firsthand, what God was doing and to meet some of the most courageous Christians I had ever met. They said they would like to do that–someday.

I looked around at the CMA members who were milling all over the campsite and noticed they were dressed…well, very casual. I had arrived in business slacks and a sport shirt and had a suit in my luggage for the evening presentation. It was a bit embarrassing to ask, but I ventured the question, "How should I dress for the meeting?" I think Herbie was the one who chuckled and responded, "Let me tell it to you this way, Bob. If our members want to really impress you, they will change their t-shirt for the evening meeting." I smiled and immediately thought, 'I don't own anything that casual!'

My drive into town took only ten minutes from the campsite. My motel room looked quite inviting and the air-conditioning was a wonderful relief from the 90+ degree meeting with the Shreves. Unpacking was almost comical since there was nothing, except my underwear, that I could wear for the evening meeting. My search for a clothing store in Williams was unfruitful. I did find a store that carried some blue jeans, so I purchased the jeans, a golf shirt, some white tennis shoes, and some white gym socks. I thought I was set for the event.

I arrived back at the campsite around 3 p.m. just to hang out with other CMA members. Everyone was very cordial and welcoming. There wasn't an unfriendly face in the crowd. I was sure my staff had greatly misjudged this group and it was going to be my pleasure to rub it in when I got back to the office.

Although I still felt a little overdressed I tried to blend in. My new dark jeans seemed to stand out, but my white tennis shoes almost blinded me when I looked around at other people's shoes. I made a mental note: wear black tennis shoes or boots next time.

As I prepared for the evening meeting, I felt that since I represented Open Doors, I should dress in the same manner I would at any other important meeting. My suit and tie were obviously out of place, but I told myself this was an important meeting and I was okay.

As the worship service began, the music was electrifying and upbeat. Herbie led worship songs and another man, Dan Fitzpatrick, led congregational songs and sang a solo. It was not like any "church" I had been to in California. I liked the sweet spirit among the people.

Herb later took the podium to speak about a new program they had just introduced called Run for the Son. He explained purpose of RFS and named the two ministries to receive checks which represented 60% of the proceeds. MVI received a $40,000 check. As I was preparing to receive the check for Open Doors, Herb explained that there were some extra collections done around the campground before the evening event so the checks could be in round figures. He then gave me a check for $80,000 for Open Doors to purchase Bibles for Christians in persecuted countries.

I took a step back, truly amazed and humbled. My thoughts ran back to the office humor and what they thought I might experience. This was the second largest single gift Open Doors had ever received. It represented almost 20,000

Bibles and it answered a major prayer for that summer. The summer months were always low for ministries and this gift gave Open Doors an adrenaline rush. I stayed around the campground as long as I could to thank everyone I met. I thanked Herb and Herbie for their vision and commitment to introduce this kind of campaign to support other ministries. I told them I could probably count on one hand the number of ministries that give money to other ministries to help with their outreach.

We stayed together holding late-night conversations about where this money would go and when some of them might be able to take a trip to China or Cuba or some other place so they could bring back a first-hand report on CMA's gift at work. That fall, Herbie and his wife traveled to China with me and visited the Great Wall and the ancient city of Shanghai. They met with house-church pastors and they listened to what God was doing in China. Herb traveled with me to Cuba the next year to visit pastors in the southern-most part of Cuba where very few Americans have gone. It was a life-changing trip for him.

That weekend visit to Williams, Arizona, to meet with a bunch of bikers changed my life and my attitude about motor-cyclists. I became a member of CMA the next year.

SECTION THREE:

Encouragement from CMA National Leadership

Run for the Son and Me

Earl Ray Burns, Board of Directors, Christian Motorcyclists Association, CMA No. 12,753

On Sunday morning, May 15, 1983, a CMAer by the name of Clare Curtis came to visit our church in Silver Lake, Kansas. He was riding a small Honda motorcycle. Our pastor, Brother Frank Claiborne, had invited Clare to talk about the Christian Motorcyclists Association and the local chapter, Heaven on Wheels, CMA Chapter #48, in Topeka. Clare gave out *Heart-Beat* papers and CMA applications. I sent in our CMA application the next day.

After church on Sunday night, my wife Marian and I met two CMAers who were members of the local chapter. We started attending their meetings, but I didn't get really involved for about two years, as I was heavily involved in the ministries of our church.

Once I became active in the chapter, I served as vice-president in 1986 and served for three years as president beginning in 1987. It was while I was serving as president of Heaven on Wheels that I attended a Changing of the Colors Rally in Hatfield, Arkansas, and heard Herbie Shreve tell of his vision for CMA to have a Run for the Son fundraiser. I was excited about it, but I was raised in a Southern Baptist Church, and Southern Baptists didn't believe in special fundraisers; we believed God's work should be carried on with tithes and offerings. My favorite scripture is Malachi 3:8-11. God honors His Word and He had proved to me over and over that being honest with God is the only way to live a happy life. I have made those verses a model for my life.

I called CMA President Herbie Shreve on two different occasions to ask him how I could serve as a CMA chapter president and support RFS when I didn't think fundraising was right. Herbie asked me to pray about it, which I did, and he prayed for me about it. I had a high respect for Herbie and considered him a very close friend and a dynamic man of God.

I didn't do much for RFS for the first two years. Then a God-thing happened in my life. I worked for the then Atchison, Topeka, and Santa Fe Railway Company in Topeka, Kansas. I worked indirectly with a man by the name of Billy Joe Heath; he and I had worked together in the superintendent's office in Temple, Texas, for a number of years. God blessed Billy Joe and he went through the ranks to become vice-president and general manager of the Atchison, Topeka, and Santa Fe. I was transferred from Temple, Texas, to Topeka, Kansas, in 1972, to help start the Centralized Timekeeping Bureau where I worked as a timekeeper until my retirement in 1997.

I contacted Billy Joe the third year of RFS and he gave me a $20 bill, which was a good gift. I contacted Billy Joe the next year about supporting me and again he gave me another $20. The next year I called Billy Joe and asked him if he would support me again. I said to Billy Joe, "I thought you were going to move back to Salado, Texas, when you retired." (Billy Joe was a golfer and I knew that he wanted to retire to the nice golf course in Salado.) Billy Joe told me he was indeed planning to move to Salado, but he had to wait until his house in Topeka sold. I told Billy Joe I really believed in prayer and I was going to pray for him that God would send him a buyer for his house. His house in Topeka was very expensive. I sent him information about RFS and a short note telling him I would be praying for God to send someone to buy his house. I expected Billy Joe to send me another check for $20. Eight days later an excited Billy Joe called me. He was in tears over what God had done—someone had come to his house that morning and paid him cash for it. Billy Joe believed it was divine intervention from God and the answer to my prayer. Praise the Lord! Billy Joe said he was going to give whoever sold his house a check for $1,500 and he was going to send it to me for RFS; I received the check the next morning. From that point in my life, I truly believed God was in the real estate business. It changed my heart and life. I have continued to

26

pray for Billy Joe all through the years since that event in our lives. Billy Joe sent me $2,500 the next year and has faithfully supported me all the years since.

As we all know, God has been blessing RFS more and more each year to where we raised $3,405,221.03 in 2006. To this day I continue to try to raise all I can, spending days during January, February, March, and April each year writing letters, etc., and in prayer for all who support our effort. I try to convey what CMA does with the money: we give 20% each to Missionary Ventures International, Open Doors, and The JESUS Film Project, and we use 40% in the United States for home missions.

RFS is one of the greatest things CMA does. God will continue to bless it more each year, as we remain faithful to Him and allow the Holy Spirit to lead us.

It is not about me; it is all about God and how He wants me to live. I'll read my Bible, pray, witness, and give, because it's not about me; it's all about God and how He wants me to live!

A Mission Trip I'll Never Forget

Eileen Upp, National, Christian Motorcyclists Association, CMA No. 34,958

In 2002 my husband, Chet, and I had the privilege to go on a mission trip to Honduras. We were part of a team led by Roger and Rayleen Wilson, CMA National Evangelists–North Central Region. I had never been on a trip with them before, but had heard stories about what to expect. I wasn't disappointed! We saw miraculous things take place.

At one of the churches we attended, very early in the prayer time, a young woman, who had her young son with her, came forward for prayer. She had been dabbling in voodoo and witchcraft. Roger prayed with this young woman possessed by a demon. As Roger finished his prayer, he signaled for Chet and me to come and take her aside to continue praying. We led her to the side to pray with her. This woman was crying and was obviously distraught and bothered by whatever was happening. I don't speak or understand Spanish, but I knew she was very involved in whatever was going on in her life and so we began to pray, and pray, and pray. As we prayed, she began to wretch, utter guttural sounds–the kinds of things you see in the movies, but aren't sure they are real. They are real! Eventually she fell to the ground and began to tremble and we continued to pray.

The pastor of the church was standing behind us and watched what was taking place. He came over and I asked him if she was ill. I still had no idea what was happening to her. He told me she was heavily into voodoo and witchcraft and the church had been praying for her for a long time. So he knelt down and began to pray with us for her.

The demon came out of her. When she stood up her face was like the face of an angel...total peace, total submission to Christ. This thing that had been bothering her was gone. Her little boy, who had been very afraid, grabbed her arm and hugged his momma.

We gave the woman a Bible and she went off and sat at the side of the church. She was a new creation! I was elated to be able to minister to this lady.

Had I never gotten involved with RFS, I would never have gone on a mission trip and would never have participated in the things God has allowed me. I never could have ministered to this woman and seen what God can do. RFS is a passion for me and I will never stop talking about it or trying to do more to see the gospel spread throughout the world.

Widening Your Perspective

Curtis Clements, National/International Lead Evangelist, Christian Motorcyclists Association, CMA No. 2,088

My wife Carole and I joined CMA in 1979, several years before the inception of RFS. Our 20-year celebration of RFS brings several things to mind.

Prior to RFS, members of CMA (including me) had a narrow view of their world. The vision of our organization is *changing the world, one heart at a time.* However, our world consisted of the United States. Most of us were of the opinion all our resources should be going to ministry to bikers in the United States only. Our concept was that mission trips and ministry in other parts of the world should be conducted by churches with their members participating in evangelism and building churches. We were happy with that concept.

When CMA appointed me as a national evangelist in 1988, I did very little for RFS and did not *want* to go on any mission trips. In 1992, when I became a regional evangelist, I still had no desire to go on mission trips, but I decided I would wholeheartedly promote RFS. I wasn't afraid to go to other countries, but at that time I just didn't know if I believed we should be spending funds in that direction. I guess I forgot Matthew 28:19 and Mark 16:15. I certainly didn't realize how much more God would bless CMA if we reached outside ourselves.

Looking back, I remember before RFS there was not enough money coming in from general donations and goodie sales to do a lot of ministry, even in the United States. We didn't have the abundance of tracts and ministry tools we have today. But the Lord blessed the small amount we received. Once RFS began and members started going on mission trips to other countries, we started hearing stories of life-changing events, both in the lives of those who went and those to whom they ministered.

The Lord spoke to me, "I'm doing something great here, and you're not going with Me?" So I thought, 'I'll go just one time and see what this is all about.' That first trip lit an inextinguishable fire in me.

There is no way to explain the joy of seeing people from other countries come to the saving knowledge of Jesus Christ—people who don't even speak our language. I now realize the love of Jesus speaks volumes in any language. I have seen physical healings, family healings, spiritual healings, as well as demonic deliverances.

There has been a complete turnaround in CMA's vision of *changing the world, one heart at a time*. Our perspective has enlarged to more than the United States. Each year, many of our active members take mission trips into countries all over the world, returning to say, "I'll never be the same."

The small motorcycles we give away through MVI change the lives of the pastors who receive them in ways we will know only in eternity. Thousands of churches have been planted with untold numbers saved. The Bibles that have gone into closed countries through Open Doors have impacted hundreds of thousands of people all across the world. We have seen millions saved through the showing of the *JESUS* film. What is happening is so big it's hard to put into words. But I do know the ministry of CMA in the United States and around the world is exploding.

In addition to outreach in other countries, this great tool, RFS, has also provided the means (40% of RFS funds are used here in the United States) to have large quantities of tracts and ministry tools printed for our members who are involved in ministry here at "home."

I thank the Lord for giving our Board of Directors a world vision and I am grateful they had enough faith to begin this great journey we call RFS. I am blessed to be a part of it and will continue as long as the Lord allows me to participate.

Choosing Change

Gary Wadding, National Evangelist–Southeast Region,
Christian Motorcyclists Association, CMA No. 10,855

I have made many CMA RFS mission trips, and my heart is full of powerful memories that will never grow dim. However, I have to confess when RFS first began, I was more concerned about how I could possibly fit a one-week foreign trip into my already impossible schedule. The main mission of my life was to reach the unsaved bikers of the United States, not to go live in a jungle somewhere and give a couple of bikes to people I didn't know. I had been a CMA lay evangelist for some years before becoming a national evangelist. Back then that meant Vicky and I were out almost constantly at secular biking events where we had built hundreds of personal relationships with men and women who were going to Hell unless somebody could reach them for Jesus. We bought into the concept of RFS, but we really didn't see it for all it was going to become to us. It took several mission trips before I realized that as American Christians we were some of the most self-centered people on earth. We have more preachers, churches, Bibles, and gospel TV/radio programs than all the rest of the world put together, several times over. There are very few in this country who can say they have not heard the gospel time after time; however, billions across the world have never heard about the Savior even once. I finally heard Jesus' call to go first to my Jerusalem, but not to forget my Judea, Samaria, and the ends of the earth.

I still have a real heart for the lost in my home country, but now I also remember those who are dying in remote nations without anybody taking Jesus to their villages. I can't go to all of them; I don't have enough time, I don't have the language skills, and I don't have the cultural understanding. But I can certainly mention this need and this wonderful outreach opportunity to my friends in order to raise funds to help them. I can certainly pray for RFS and ask the Lord to send funds our way.

Those foreign pastors give all they have, and many are daily in danger of losing their lives for the sake of the gospel. They have taught me more about faith and Christian service than all the books I have ever read. I am ashamed to have ever wondered why we should give a tiny portion of our abundance to help them get transportation, or Bibles, or see the *JESUS* film.

I remember Bernard in Africa who walks on as many of his trips as he can, to save the motorcycle for the longer trips. He views his motorcycle as a holy gift from God, and won't use it as a toy or hobby. How many of us would be willing to do that? Bernard had to quit school after the sixth grade due to poverty, but he has educated himself and also has wisdom that comes only from God. Those to whom he ministers are blessed, and we had a part in getting him to them on a CMA RFS dirt bike.

I know one man who still walks everywhere and hops a passing truck or bus to get around. He could have a bike, but he refers them on to others in order to bless them. I've seen children by the hundreds rush this man just to touch him and look him in the eye while he smiles and tells them Jesus loves them. When I've walked with this particular man in Haiti, I literally felt as though I were walking with Jesus across Galilee. I come home humbled every time I spend time with such people. My heart has been changed from the first time I heard about RFS. Praise God for His mercy to me.

As a Vietnam veteran, my heart often goes back to that country where I had been responsible for the deaths of so many men who faced me in combat. I began to look into the possibility of taking a mission trip back there. The problems were considerable. The danger was real. The Communist government was harsh in its treatment of Vietnamese who were in contact with westerners. We had to meet with pastors secretly, at great danger to them. We couldn't get anybody a nice new motorbike because it would draw too much attention.

33

Their bike would be confiscated and these faithful men and women would be put in jail. We finally arranged for a Vietnamese intermediary to buy several old bikes, and then have them rebuilt completely on the inside while leaving the outside looking beat up. Later he secretly transferred these gifts to the needy pastors who could now use them safely. One emaciated assistant pastor humbly told me his youngest son had been praying for three years that his daddy would get a bicycle to help him travel and tell people about Jesus. Several times on that trip the Vietnamese Christians risked prison to protect us from danger. I was in awe of their faith and love for Christ and us, in light of the fact that we had been there a few years ago in wartime. One man cautiously came up to me on the crowded streets of Saigon and asked me if I had been there during the war. I said that I had been. He told me, "When you go back home, tell those other men thanks for trying." Then he silently slipped back into the crowd to avoid being seen. I felt such love on this trip I began to consider whether I could possibly stay and give everything I had to these amazing people. I know I would have attracted too much attention and been of little real use, but if I had not been married with a family, the temptation would have been very hard to resist. I felt the love of God for the Vietnamese people like none others I have ever visited. I will never be the same.

I want you to look into Jesus' eyes and see the reflection of so many saints in so many places who are praying to Him for help in reaching their fellow countrymen with the gospel, just the way we all want to do here in America. We don't have an "either-or" choice. We can do both through CMA and RFS. Pray and let God use you to *change the world, one heart at a time.*

God Grants the Desires of the Righteous

Vicky Wadding, National–Southeast Region, Christian Motor-cyclists Association, CMA No. 10,856

When CMA began RFS, I thought they had lost it. We had never been about money. We had never asked our members to give, much less to collect from others. I was definitely out of my comfort zone. But though I didn't like the method, the cause seemed worthy.

RFS was designed to help other ministries and individuals do the same thing CMA was doing. We would give instead of just receive; I liked that. Also, I didn't want to appear outwardly rebellious to our leadership, so as we began this project Gary and I would donate the required amount to get a t-shirt, at that time it was $50. For years that was what RFS meant to me.

In 1991, my husband and I came on staff and began to catch the vision of RFS. We saw how local pastors in many countries were helped with their own motorcycles. Now they could be at home with their families more instead of walking miles and miles. Now they could reach more people with the gospel because they could go farther in a shorter amount of time. I even got to meet some of these pastors and their families by going on mission trips with CMA.

I realized how many could now get Bibles that never could before and how many more souls could be saved. My eyes were opened and I put a lot more into RFS. Every year we would collect between $1,000 and $1,500. That was a big increase over what we had done before. It was our best effort.

What I want to tell you about is what happened to me in early 1996. We were at a staff meeting and we were shown the incentives for the 1997 RFS. I don't know what happened to me. I had never been motivated by these incentives before, but that year they had made a special gold CMA ring for the $5,000 incentive, and it caught my eye.

35

I told Gary, "I want one of those rings," but he just laughed. We both knew we were giving it our best effort already and hadn't been able to come near the $5,000 mark. One morning while doing my devotions I read Proverbs 10:24, *What the wicked dreads will overtake him; what the righteous desire will be granted.*

Of course, I knew that because of Jesus I was righteous. But it seemed my desires were too big and not worthy to be fulfilled. But I heard the Lord whispering, "It is no big deal." Did He actually mean I could have that ring? Well, long story short, for RFS 1997, we raised $5,000, earned the gold ring, and–of all things–placed sixth place in the nation. As we were on stage to receive our award, they asked the gentleman who was in first place (Director Ray Burns) how he did it. His answer was simple: "I just told the Lord I wanted to do more." I thought to myself, "What did **you** say, Vicky?" I just wanted the gold ring.

The events of that year changed me forever. I now knew for certain God does miracles for us today. It was a miracle to jump from $1,500 to $5,000. From that point until today, every year I say, "Lord, I want to do more." And I can do more now that I have learned the secret for fundraising: 1 Thessalonians 5:24, *The one who calls you is faithful and he will do it.* He has continued to fulfill my desires. He wants to do miraculous things through CMA and us as individuals. He is pleased with our complete trust in Him, and our complete faith in His Word.

How about it…what do you want?

Seeing the Heart behind the Effort

Rick Steffy, National Evangelist–Northeast Region, Christian Motorcyclists Association, CMA No. 28,824

Run for the Son is about more than raising money. Have you ever gone on the vacation of your dreams, only to return home feeling empty and wondering who really benefited from all the money you spent? You can be certain of this: If you choose to go on an RFS mission trip, you will return home with a sense of fulfillment. Sharing ourselves with those less fortunate helps us take our eyes off ourselves.

These trips are about opening your heart to the needs of others, with the extra benefit of meeting CMA members from other states. You get to experience the true culture of a foreign country, seeing God work in ways you never would expect. For example, when we were in the Philippines, one night at an outdoor crusade we saw a large group of over 80 people come forward to receive Christ as their Savior.

In Argentina, my wife Eileen prayed for a woman with marital problems; yes, they have the same problems we do in America. I prayed for a woman who was tormented by spirits and she was delivered right there on the spot. Every trip is special. It is really impossible to pinpoint any one special incident, or one trip that is more memorable than another. It is more about what happens within the hearts of those who go on the trips. Some of us think only those individuals with special training or outstanding talents could go on mission trips. But thanks to CMA's connection with our ministry partners, this thought is not true. We are all capable of touching lives around the world. I feel honored that God has allowed me to be a part of this great missionary endeavor.

Our Brother's Keeper

Roger Wilson, National Evangelist–North Central Region, Christian Motorcyclists Association, CMA No. 32,935

Run for the Son, what can I say? God knew what needed to be done and CMA stepped up to the plate.

On our first RFS ride, my wife Rayleen and I were not sure it was something we, as CMA, should be doing. After all, we were a motorcyclist outfit with ministry in the United States; what should we have to do with raising money for overseas missions? But, we figured that if God was in it, we needed to be a part of it, and a part of it we are! We saw after that first year CMA *did* have a calling to reach out to people around the world. We knew even though we could not go, there were people who could–our ministry partners.

The third year of RFS, Rayleen and I decided it was time to really get involved. We were part of a forming chapter in Kansas and we encouraged the members to raise money for RFS. That year our forming chapter and I received recognition for being the second highest fund-raising chapter and second highest fund-raising member in the nation.

The next year we went with Herbie Shreve on a mission trip to Guatemala and Nicaragua. That trip changed us and we have never looked back. Over the years, RFS has changed in size and more people have caught the same vision Rayleen and I caught on that mission trip. We want to be there for our brothers and sisters around the world and God has provided us a way through RFS. RFS is God's plan. We encourage everyone in CMA to spread God's Word around the world through Missionary Ventures International, Open Doors, and The JESUS Film Project. We are our brother's keeper.

Effective Prayers of a Righteous Man

Joe Maxwell, National Evangelist–Northwest Region, Christian Motorcyclists Association, CMA No. 11,671

Each year Judy and I have the privilege to be part of a mission team whose purpose is to deliver motorcycles to pastors in third world countries. Each mission trip holds special memories as we see God's hand present in leading, guiding, and planning them. As special as each trip is, there is one that seems to stand out.

In 2003, we were scheduled to go to the Philippines. We looked forward to the trip and were excited about visiting a place I had been a few years previous. As we made preparations, there seemed to be a check as to whether this was to be our destination. Our desire was to go to the Philippines; however, we thought that maybe this was not the year. Possibly, there was a different place God had in mind. I contacted Missy Parmenter, the CMA contact for mission trips, and shared my thoughts. I asked her to contact MVI to find out if there was a need at a different location. When she called me back, she asked if I would consider going to the Dominican Republic. The Dominican Republic had never crossed my mind. She expressed the need and said a team had not been there. So, I thought that possibly, God was in this. We changed our destination and shared the information through the *HeartBeat*. We quickly filled the trip with CMA members ready to go to the Dominican Republic, with a possible venture into Haiti. While we were making preparations, we had no knowledge this was a result of the prayers of a missionary from Uruguay.

We arrived in Santiago, Dominican Republic and a couple of days later we traveled to Dajabon, Dominican Republic. Dajabon is on the border of the Dominican Republic and Haiti. It was here that we met Pastor Miguel Campos and his wife, Anna, missionaries from Uruguay.

Pastor Miguel had been working with the national pastors in Haiti for a number of years. He saw, firsthand, the poverty and conditions that existed. He understood the need of the people and he also realized the need of the pastors, especially those in Haiti.

There was one pastor he worked with who had been a pastor for thirty-eight years. His only mode of transportation was walking or riding on the back of a small, 125cc motorcycle taxi. However, that ride was most often too costly. So, Pastor Miguel started praying for transportation for this pastor. Pastor Miguel did not know about CMA and RFS. But, he knew God and believed God was able to supply transportation for this pastor. Consequently, not just one Haitian pastor received a motorcycle that year, but there were three delivered, two on this trip and one a few months later.

Jesus tells us in Luke 11:9, *Ask and it will be given to you.*

Do You Know Where Your Socks Are?

Hiram Villaseñor, National Evangelist–Southwest Region,
Christian Motorcyclists Association, CMA No. 57,499

In the last nine years, I have gone on eight RFS mission trips with MVI. Each time I went, whether as a team member, or now as a team leader, I came back without any socks, because they had been blessed off!

In Honduras, we took a bus to a village a couple of hours out of town. In the middle of nowhere, we stopped on the side of the road, got off the bus, and walked down a narrow trail until we arrived at the village. We carried shoes for the kids and tried, sometimes without success, to fit them with new shoes. Some of these children had never had a pair of shoes on and they didn't like them!

Before we left, the pastor asked if they could offer us something to drink. They brought out glasses of soda with *ICE!* To this day, I don't understand how they had ice in that remote little village because to the best of my knowledge, there was no electricity there. Ice had to be a very special thing for them and they gave it to us! These folks had nothing compared to what we have, but they gave us the best they had. I came home without ANY socks from that trip!

Before our trip to Arequipa, Peru, Jim Brannon, the MVI field coordinator, asked us if we would be interested in doing a construction project: putting a new roof on a young couple's home. They were expecting a baby and they needed the new roof before the rainy season came. We accepted the project. Jim sent me a picture of their house so I could get an idea of what would be involved. The picture showed a pile of rocks with pieces of corrugated tin for a roof, held down with rocks and tires. There was no way to attach a new roof to that structure. When we got to Peru, the pile of rocks and tin were gone and we built them a 10'x12' blockhouse. We laid the block, put the roof on, and poured a concrete floor all in the

41

short week we were there. We worked hard, got some bumps and bruises, but you would have thought we had built them a mansion. That young couple had the best-looking, sturdiest, most weather-proof house in the neighborhood. To this day, I still remember the looks on their faces and the tears they shed! Once again, my socks were gone!

By far, the most diverse trip we have made was the trip we took in November 2006, to Puerto Maldonado, Peru. We were there the year before and had talked with Jim Brannon about the motorcycles in the town. About 90% of the vehicles in this jungle town are little 100–150cc motorcycles. Jim had the idea to hold a motorcycle rally. Nothing like that had ever taken place there.

Jim got some of the local churches to work together and the event was a huge success. We had a crusade one night on the street right outside the city's market and about forty folks accepted the Lord. After it was over, Jim invited all the pastors who had worked with the motorcycle rally and crusade to join us for lunch. This was the first time these pastors had ever done anything together as an outreach for their community. Jim asked me to speak to the group, so I shared about CMA. They were amazed that we were such a big organization, but what surprised them most was when I explained to them that we were from many different denominations. I told them we didn't focus on our differences; we focused on our common belief in Jesus Christ and His atonement for our sins. That was a totally new concept for them. They caught a glimpse of what can happen when we, as the body of Christ, move beyond our differences and focus on doing something for the cause of Christ. Just the thought of these pastors catching that vision and running with it brings about a new chapter in the spiritual atmosphere in Puerto Maldonado, Peru!

Whether you are considering going on your first short-term mission trip or if you have gone on a hundred, God will always do something unforgettable. Just GO! I promise you, you'll have to go to the store and buy some more SOCKS!

Life-Long Dream of Mission Trip Comes True

Sharon Villaseñor, National–Southwest Region, Christian Motorcyclists Association, CMA No. 57, 500

We were going to Nicaragua! It was exciting to prepare for this mission trip that had been a life-long dream of mine. When I was a little girl, I had prayed many times, "Lord, I will go anywhere you want me to go and do anything You want me to do." I thought I would become a missionary to Africa, China, India, or some other foreign country.

But, after graduating from high school, I married a wonderful young Christian man that God had brought into my life. Hiram and I had been friends in our church youth group. Right before we married and shortly after we were married, I had two dreams in which I saw Hiram speaking in Spanish to a group of people in some Hispanic country. Both times the dreams were identical: same place, same people, same everything! When I told Hiram about the dreams, on both occasions He told me, "That will never happen!" So I just put my dreams on a shelf in the back of my mind and really didn't think much about them again.

In 1995, Hiram and I joined CMA. We needed something we both liked to do that would bring us together. I had devoted my life to the task of home schooling our three daughters, while Hiram had focused on building Daystar Construction Company. Our lives had grown apart even though we still had Jesus as common ground.

In 1997, Hiram became the CMA New Mexico State Coordinator, and in 1998, he won a trip from MVI for raising the most RFS funds in the Southwest region. He chose to go to Nicaragua, and of course, I was going with him! A week before we were to leave, Hurricane Mitch hit many Central American countries; Nicaragua had been hit hard. I called MVI to see how things were and if we were still going to be able to go there. They said, the trip was still on, but we would need to

43

change the nature of it somewhat. We needed to bring supplies and food of a certain kind. So we got on the phone and began contacting those who could help us.

In Nicaragua, we visited the dump, taking food, medical supplies, and gifts for the children. As we gave out the gifts to the children, I was mobbed and they almost pulled my skirt off because they were so desperate. We worked side by side with nurses dispensing medicine to the families. Because so many medical teams were in Nicaragua, all the interpreters were busy and we didn't have one for our team. Hiram was the only one on our team who spoke Spanish, so he spent all day interpreting for us and for some doctors. After working with and feeding the children, I spent the rest of the day with the nurses, giving out worming medicine and treating impetigo.

The next day we went to a place that had been divided into small lots where people could build themselves some kind of shelter. The government had provided them with a few pieces of wood, wire, tin, and black plastic. Our team helped build these "houses" all day long. Hiram was busy interpreting while I passed out medication and prayed for moms and children. One nurse got upset at me and told me to wash my hands and to quit kissing all of the children because of lice and other diseases. I told her I wouldn't catch anything, but I did what she asked.

Sunday we presented a motorcycle at a church in the capital city of Managua. When we arrived there, we found a man asleep on the bench inside the church. No one else was there yet. This was the pastor who was to receive the bike and he thought he was a day late. He had been hitchhiking and walking from the mountains for several days to get to the city after the hurricane. We assured him he was not too late and that we were the ones with his bike.

Hiram interpreted the service while I took pictures and videotaped. As I panned across the room, I realized this was the fulfillment of the dreams that I had twenty-seven years earlier! The place and the faces were the same as in the dreams and Hiram was speaking in Spanish! I was so excited

I stood up and dropped the camera that was on my lap. Never discount a dream from God that is exactly the same two or three times in a row!

After the service, we had an opportunity to speak with the pastor that received the motorcycle. He was over thirty small churches that ministered to the Mosquito Indians. When we asked him if he was going to ride his new motorcycle home, he told us it would be impossible for at least a month due to the road conditions. We asked our MVI field coordinator if there was another way for him to get his bike home and she said the only way was for him to put it on a plane and fly home. That would cost him about a year's salary and he could not afford it. Our team "passed the hat" and received enough to fly him and his bike home. When we returned home, we shared our story with our CMA chapter and they took up an offering for the pastor and his family.

This mission trip changed my life forever.

Challenge of a Lifetime

Randal Tebeau, National Evangelist–Special Projects, Christian Motorcyclists Association, CMA No. 55,731

It was hard to imagine everything that was racing through my mind as I was sitting on the plane heading back to the United States. Our CMA mission team was headed home from Guatemala after a great trip. The experiences during my first mission trip out of the United States were moving and touched my heart in places that had not been touched before. The people we met and worked with painted a face of Jesus that I had never seen.

We delivered three RFS bikes to some of the most humble servants of Christ. Tears flowed with the provisions God had made. We worked on a MVI-sponsored hospital, giving it a new coat of paint, fixing the lights so they actually worked, and repairing their backup generator. This gave Dr. Pabel a new glow as he worked with patients who were in desperate need of medical attention. We gave a love offering to a young man to provide critically needed medicine and care to keep his wife, the mother of their children, alive. His face was priceless. We had a special time of prayer with a local pastor who had an inner-city church that ministered to drug and alcohol addicted folks and street gangs. The unity of our team, even with our many differences, was certainly God-ordained.

As I sat there looking out the window of the plane, I couldn't help but think back to where RFS had started for me and just how much it impacted and changed me. I thought back to my first RFS in 1996 when I rode up to our starting location at the Harley dealership. A handful of us gathered to pray and head out on our 100-mile ride. WOW, 100 miles! I was looking forward to a big day of riding on that long trip, but it wasn't meant to be! As I thumbed the starter button, my Harley just grunted and wouldn't start. After getting a push to get her going I wished the other CMA folks a good day and headed home a little disappointed at not being able to make the ride. Oh well, I had given enough money to make sure Lisa and I got one of the RFS shirts. We could always use another shirt!

The next few years saw quite a progression in our local RFS ride. Our chapter (Glory Riders, Savannah, GA) decided to invite bikers from the other local groups to join us on our ride. Each member gathered door prizes and food for the riders from local businesses all the while sharing about RFS. We handed out flyers inviting everyone to ride with us. We planned exciting routes and handed out maps so riders could really enjoy what riding a bike was all about. At the end of the ride, we gave out the door prizes and enjoyed the free food! Of course, donations for the RFS were accepted, but there was no pressure. The ride numbers grew steadily over the years and peaked out at over 250 riders one year, quite a difference from the original handful of CMA members that first year. This helped the chapter raise funds for RFS, but it also helped build relationships in the local biking community that opened doors of opportunity to minister and share Christ.

When a few folks from the Savannah chapter started a forming chapter in Statesboro, Georgia, they continued in this same tradition. The new Redeemed Riders chapter partici-pated with the Savannah chapter a couple of years before beginning their own RFS ride. The fundraising results for RFS were obvious and the impact to ministry opportunities in the local biking groups increased. We promoted this RFS ride information among our Georgia chapters, and many did the same thing, with some variation, in their own areas.

Over these early years there were many memorable and special moments that popped into my mind:

Coco, the leader of a local club, asked me if he could ride sweep along with me during the ride one year. It was quite a change from the first time we met. We were at a secular event when Coco had come by our CMA booth to check us out, to see if we were for real. Our relationship grew from that original meeting and doors opened for CMA to minister to this group. Later that same year, at Coco's funeral I was able to share with his parents the good news that he had had a relationship with Christ.

Then there was the time at the local HOG chapter meeting when my wife, Lisa, and I volunteered to take care of the 50-50 tickets after the person who usually took care of it didn't make the meeting. We just happened to have a roll of door prize tickets with us that we planned to use during the RFS in a few weeks. As we were working through the members, one man handed me a $100 bill and said, "This is for your Run for the Son." I sometimes wonder if he would have donated that to us if we hadn't been handling the 50-50. As the meeting drew to a close the director announced that the 50-50 proceeds would go to a special charity this month, CMA's RFS. We were pretty ecstatic that they would do this for CMA. The surprises didn't stop there; when they called the winning ticket number, I had it in my hand! It was quite humorous to hear the folks jokingly talk about how it was all rigged, but they quickly stated there was no way they were going to argue with God, who had set this up. I informed the folks that *all* the money would go to RFS–a total of over $400–and a great applause filled the room.

A few years ago, I stood hand in hand with over 100 CMA members as we prayed for RFS. Members from several chapters in Georgia and Tennessee had their RFS rides end at the Fields of the Wood in Tennessee, a place where the Ten Commandments lay in stone on the side of a mountain. We enjoyed hamburgers, hotdogs, and all the fixings–quite a picnic with great fellowship to boot. Even here, there was a special love offering taken and given to help support the ministry of the place where we gathered.

I remembered back to the time I heard Vicky Wadding talk about RFS and how she and Gary had decided to donate any extra money they received. Well, I had heard this before, but Lisa and I finally felt led to do the same thing. I didn't expect things to change a lot, because we never had folks give us any extra money. That year things did change and the very next year I was a top ten RFS fundraiser. This gave me the opportunity to go on my first mission trip!

As I watched the city of Guatemala disappear from sight, I could understand a part of the impact the CMA Run for the Son makes for Jesus in this world. On a deeper, personal level, I could understand the impact RFS makes in CMA members, chapters, and the biking community. Yes, this has been quite a trip.

I'm excited to see what God has in store for each of us as CMA celebrates the 20th anniversary of RFS. The prayer is for 20,000 members to participate in RFS during this special time. Will you take the challenge and see just where God takes you?

God-Directed Path

Holly Ogden, National–Fast Lane, Christian Motorcyclists Association, CMA No. 70,387

Run for the Son touched my life in an indirect way, but with major impact. My salvation and the salvations of some of my family members are results of home missions. Usually when people go on mission trips, they spend time with people who are hurting, needing a touch from God, and needing someone to say to them, "I care." My story is no different.

My journey began in June of 1998 when my dad visited a local motorcycle dealership and informed me that they had a red 1993 Honda Nighthawk 750 for sale–the bike I had wanted since taking his motorcycle safety course in 1996. I put pen to paper to make sure I could afford to purchase the motorcycle and afford to attend college. Two days later, we picked the bike up from the dealership and a friend rode it to the local mall for me to put it into a motorcycle show (I needed a refresher course on how to operate a clutch). After we finished staging my bike, my dad asked me if I had met the CMAers that were just a few yards away from us and took me over to introduce me. From there, God radically altered the path of my life.

My first impression of Harry and Sherrie Lord was that they were very happy. I was going through a tough time in my life where I knew I was not walking the right path, but I did not know how to get off it. I battled with depression and felt like I was the most unlovable person in the world. I needed help, but did not know where to turn or who to trust.

Unwittingly, Harry and Sherrie asked me if I wanted to go on some rides with them. From that point on, I became like a part of their family. Everywhere they went, I went too. They showed me a love like none I had ever known and through this, God drew my heart back to Him, showing me He had been with me through all of the pain. I started to turn my back on my old behaviors and felt like a new person–I desired things I had never desired before and I had a new kind of hunger in my heart. Unfortunately, my group of "friends" did not understand the changes in me and kept trying to pull me back into their folds.

In the summer of 1999, we attended the CMA Tri-States State Rally. Diane Schultz (Shreve) was at the rally and for some reason, she stopped one of her conversations mid-sentence and asked me how old I was and if I was single. Then she explained to me that there was someone in Arkansas that I just needed to meet–a John Ogden, Jr.

She introduced the two of us via email and we began corresponding. Through our conversations, I learned about John having a morning devotional time–something I had never heard of before. Being competitive in nature, I figured if he could have one, then I could have one too! I embarked on a deeper walk with God as I realized that life with Him was more than just a one-time decision, it was a relationship. It was amazing to read the Bible that had remained on my shelf except for Sunday mornings.

In December of 1999, CMA offered me a position similar to what I was currently doing. John was blunt with me and told me I had better know this was God's will for my life, because if I was moving just to be close to him and we didn't work out, then I would be stuck with no family in an unfamiliar place and he was under no obligation to me. After much prayer, I decided it was time to begin a new life.

Working for CMA I have come to deeply appreciate all of the areas RFS touches and the countless testimonies of lives changed, for I am one of them. I was a mission, and God sent people into my field to plant and water seeds. He harvested my soul and most remarkably also brought in the hearts of some family members. Praise God for the Run for the Son!

SECTION FOUR:

Homeland Missions

As you read the following testimonies, please keep in mind that some may not appear to be directly related to RFS. However, it is important to understand that the RFS is an integral part of the ministry of CMA and works behind the scenes in many circumstances by providing the training materials, ministry items, and actual training to the leaders who then train the leaders in their areas.

Forever Changed by His Love

Jes Salais, Texas, CMA No. 92,801

Our story starts back in 1997 when my husband, Bear, was diagnosed with Chronic Hepatitis C. The doctors tried different treatments, but he was a non-responder. He became a test subject for every new medication they came out with, but nothing ever worked. In the end, the doctors told him they were just trying to buy him more time, but he was going to die within the next 5 years.

His job retired him, stating he was not fit for duty. Bear became very depressed. He felt he had done something really bad to make God punish him with this illness saying, "I wish I knew what I did wrong so I could ask God to forgive me." We didn't know at the time that God can do no wrong and it was the devil attacking us.

Bear turned to street drugs to dull the pain and sorrow. He was on a form of chemo that made him very sick and caused blisters when he went into the sun. I was so stressed out I quit my job and I began working at a tattoo shop (one of Bear's hobbies is tattooing). We made friends with a couple there–Cheryl and "Uncle" Bill Henderson. Cheryl amazed me with the way she handled situations at the shop (it can be a crazy place to work). She dealt with situations in a calm manner, seeing the positive side of things while having a peace about her. I wanted that peace.

As Bear sank deeper into his drugs, I was running the house, trying to pay all the bills, and caring for my disabled older sister. There were times I would feel like I couldn't go another day and I wanted to end my life–I couldn't do this all by myself!

I used some of my retirement money to get us a motorcycle, hoping it would cheer Bear up. Uncle Bill and Cheryl had invited us to go to one of their CMA chapter meetings, so we went to see what it was like. We continued to ride with Uncle

Bill and Cheryl after that first meeting, and I continued to want the peace Cheryl had.

Bear still suffered from depression, and there were times when Uncle Bill would come at 2:00 a.m. to help me when Bear was suicidal. Uncle Bill would come into the house and say, "You go to bed, Sweetie. Don't worry. Everything will be okay." He would sit in the living room with Bear, drinking coffee and talking. I would go to bed and sleep because I knew Uncle Bill was there. Cheryl and Uncle Bill loved us the way we were and made us believe there was hope.

On January 6, 2002, I asked Bear if he wanted to go for a ride after we finished our chores around the house, as it was a beautiful day. We took off just after lunch and were about 20 minutes away from the house on a beautiful, narrow road that winds around the river and hills. We were heading for a curve when a car came around on our side of the road. There was nowhere to go, as there was a guardrail on one side, a hill on the other side, and a car in front of us. I pushed myself off the back of the bike, trying to pull Bear with me. Bear ended up going down with the bike. The fall knocked me out.

When I came to, the driver was standing over me crying and apologizing. I didn't remember what had happened until I heard Bear screaming he did not want a car to hit him. I jumped up and started running down the road to where he and the bike had landed. The headlight of the bike was touching his helmet, and his leg was turned in an unnatural direction. I calmed him down telling him other bikers had stopped and were not letting traffic through. The bikers came and helped me move him to the side of the road. Long story short the ambulance came and took Bear to the hospital. The three bikers that had stopped offered to take our bike (not a scratch on it) and me home so I could get our truck and go to the hospital.

Once there I called Uncle Bill and Cheryl, who came to the emergency room and prayed with Bear. In the days that followed there were many visitors to Bear's room wearing CMA patches on their backs. We didn't know who they all were, but they sat with Bear and gave me time to care for my sister and change my clothes. They brought me food and loved on us.

Bear came home from the hospital, and this time he was not only using street drugs, he now had prescription drugs. He sank deeper into his depression. The doctors had put an external fixation on Bear's leg, but by August of 2005 there was still no bone growth. The doctors told him it would never heal to where it would be usable, so Bear asked them to remove it.

The day of the surgery Cheryl came and stayed all day. After the surgery, Bear was fine until the anesthesia wore off. He then got out of bed and hopped down the hall on his remaining leg, while holding onto his IV pole, screaming he had made a mistake and asking the people he passed to kill him—he couldn't stand the pain. Cheryl helped me get him back into his bed. She wiped his face with a washcloth, and spoke softly to him. I was crying as I sat across the bed from her. I calmed down and started to listen to her—she was praying and Bear was falling asleep. I *really* wanted her peace.

She came every day and sat with us. Uncle Bill and other CMAers continued to come, and whenever they were there, Bear was calm—he could handle the pain as they prayed and loved on us. There was a housekeeping lady at the hospital that would clean his room, then take off her gloves and lay her hands on Bear's face, praying with him for a peaceful sleep and healing. On the days she came in, he would sleep most of the night.

Bear came home from his surgery after a month and a half in the hospital. He continued on his drive to kill himself. I watched church on TV on Sunday mornings, but one Sunday morning something made me get up and go check on Bear. He was in the bathroom with a needle in his arm with enough drugs to kill an elephant. He was dripping in sweat, blood was running down his arm, and his face was filled with pain. I screamed and started to cry, telling him I couldn't do this anymore. I took off my wedding rings, and went to the living room. He came to the living room crying and saying, "I didn't do it." He told me to call Uncle Bill and Cheryl. They came out and spent the day with us, loving us in spite of the things we did.

They invited us to a blessing of the bikes with the local CMA chapter, Alamo Apostles, the following week. We went and stood off to the side, taking in all the activities. Then, two men came up to us–Steve Moore and Bruce Smith. Steve looked Bear in the eye and said, "God spoke to my heart and told me I need to talk with you and pray with you." God told Steve exactly what our situation was; he knew we did not want to live or where to turn. Steve and Bruce loved on us, prayed for us, and let us see that God loved us no matter what. He also let Bear know God wasn't punishing him.

We told Steve we had tried to go to different churches in the area, but were shunned because of the way we looked. He invited us to a biker friendly church, and we told him we would check it out sometime. The following Sunday we got up, I put Bear and his wheelchair in the truck, and we went to church. It took us twenty minutes to get to our seats because of everyone hugging and loving us. The pastor made it a point every Sunday to find Bear and love on him. Bear stopped doing street drugs, but was still on prescription drugs.

After 10 months of going to this church, they announced they were opening a school of ministry. I knew nothing about God and Bear said he wanted to get more knowledge, so we enrolled in the school. During that first year of Bible school, we volunteered at a Christian coffeehouse. One night, the people singing there asked that anyone needing prayer for healing come forward. Bear didn't want to go–a lot of people had already prayed for him. The singer then called Bear up by name. All the CMAers went up and laid their hands on Bear as the lady (Joann Perez) prayed for him. I looked up at Bear during the prayer and I could see the love the CMAers had for us on their faces as they were all praying for his healing. I then looked at Bear and I saw a peace flow over him–the

59

same peace I always saw in the CMA people–his whole being changed, he had color in his face. I knew at that moment he had been healed! The doctor confirmed it a few months later, and they stated they had not healed Bear; it came from a higher power, God. We dedicated our lives to reaching out to others the way CMA and our church reached out to us.

We graduated from the first year of the ministry school and were licensed to preach the gospel. During that year we had grown to love God, and with the love and patience of the CMA people around us, we saw a better way of life and that God loves us as we are. Bear came off all prescription drugs.

We now go into the community to reach out and minister to the lost and hurting the way CMAers reached out to us. If it were not for the boldness of the CMAers God put in our path to step up and show us God's love and power through them, Bear and I would no longer be on this earth. There are mission fields in other countries; there is also a huge mission field all over the United States. Simple acts of kindness, love, and concern show God's light brightly in a dark place.

The Cross

Barbara Joy Hansen, Massachusetts, CMA No. 72,115

The day we participated in the RFS ride was awesome and exhilarating! We met up with Bob and Kathy Pezutto [former New England State Coordinators] and sixty-seven other bikers. After we met in our prayer circle to ask God to keep us safe and give us opportunities to be a witness for Him, we rode 130 miles together. Our destination on this sunny day to support RFS was a farm called "The Cross" in Barre, Massachusetts. An eighty-year-old farmer, John Harty, built a cross in a field in front of his house. The cement cross, built into the ground, is 200 feet long and 25 feet wide. God distinctly told John to level his farming field and make a cross out of cement with the Ten Commandments on it. John was never much for 'religion' and was skeptical at first, but he became a man of stronger faith when a friend of his was miraculously healed from a severe spinal cord injury. Then God healed John of a hearing loss thirty-six years after he shot himself in his ear at the age of seventeen. John knew that many people would come to see "The Cross" and he made his property available to those who need to hear about the love of Jesus.

One of those people was Nick, a twenty-year-old biker. I was planting flowers when Nick first came to see the Honda CB-750 custom bike we had for sale. My husband wasn't home so I showed him the bike and we sat in the grass as I easily shared my faith with him. I told him we were members of CMA. Nick told me he had grown up in a Catholic home and had not gone to confession since the age of ten. He said, "I'm not religious," and he seemed surprised when I told him, "It's not religion that we have...it is faith in Christ and a personal relationship with Him."

Nick gave my husband a deposit for the bike, but a few weeks later, he called and said, "I lost my job and can't afford to buy the bike." He told us to keep the $500 deposit, which we declined to do. He was not getting along with his parents and had just broken up with a girlfriend. Nothing was going right in his life, so we offered to hold the bike for him until he could pay for it. We told him we would pray for him and we would put the bike in our shed for the winter. He didn't know what to say. He had never seen love like this before.

Just prior to our RFS ride Nick completely paid for the motorcycle and we invited him to go with us on our trip. He was intimidated to go with a new group and wasn't sure he would be able to keep up, but we assured him it was an 'easy beginner' ride. When we got to *The Cross*, Nick asked if he could talk with me. We walked out onto the huge cross and he began to read, *I am the Lord thy God...Thou shalt have no other gods before me. Thou shalt not make unto thee any graven image...Thou shalt not take the Name of the Lord thy God in vain...Thou shalt not kill. Thou shalt not commit adultery* (Exodus 20:2-14, KJV). He said to me, "Barb, I've probably broken nearly every commandment." I told him we all have sinned and fallen short of God's glory, Romans 3:23, but God forgives our sins. Nick began to ask questions. "Is this group Catholic or Protestant?" I explained that CMA welcomes people of all faiths, and that not everyone who rides with us is a Christian yet, but many are. Some are seeking to know who God is and others are new believers. God loves him so much He died for his life. Each of us sins and is separated from God, but Jesus Christ, not 'religion' is God's only provision for our sins and each of us must personally receive Jesus by faith.

I told Nick we would continue to pray for him that God would change his life for the better. Not long after our ride I spoke with his mother. She told me things had gotten better between them. I told her that riding with us would be a good example to him and that she would continue to see positive changes in Nick. She said, "I'm gonna hold you to that!" *But God forbid that I should boast except in the cross of our Lord Jesus Christ* (Galatians 6:14, NKJV).

True Colors

Karan Lapham, Montana, CMA No. 61,537

As my husband, Jeff, and I were returning to Montana from the October 2005 Changing of the Colors 30th Anniversary International Rally, we stopped for lunch in a little home-owned café in the small town of Carrizozo, New Mexico. As we were looking over the menus, the manager of the café advised us that a gentleman seated in the dining area wanted to buy our lunch.

We approached the gentleman and introduced ourselves. He explained the reason he wanted to buy our lunch is that he had seen our colors. He went on to tell us he was from Texas and was on a business trip, just stopping for lunch as we were. His nephew in Arizona, who was not walking the path he should, had met some CMAers and, as a result of their love and testimony, his life had turned around. Ours were the first colors this man had seen since speaking with his nephew. He was so impressed by what he had heard about CMA, he wanted to meet someone actually involved and learn more about the organization.

After a very enjoyable lunch, he asked how he could help support CMA's mission. As we explained RFS, he reached for his checkbook and wrote a substantial check for RFS. The manager of the café had also become involved in our conversation and she brought her father, the owner of the café, to meet us. They also gave us a check for RFS.

We first learned of CMA in 1995, participated in our first RFS in 1996, and have been active every year since. RFS is one of our biggest activities, as we go about *changing the world, one heart at a time.*

Thank you, CMA, for allowing us to be a part of this great venture.

63

Not By Accident

Joe Marchelewski, New York, CMA No. 115,466

I had been in CMA for five months before my first RFS, only riding a motorcycle for nine months total. I had wanted a motorcycle for many years, but with raising a family and working, it was not practical. I finally bought a bike in September of 2005 and shortly afterwards God told me I could have it if I used it for Him. I joined CMA and Bikers for Christ and so began my mission. It was fantastic to have fellowship with the chapter members, and to be around all these Christians who ride.

I was going to be at my brother's in Winchester, Virginia, the day of the RFS ride, so I called the local chapter and made arrangements to ride with them on the day of the Run. About twenty-five miles into the Run we were up in the mountains. Coming around a turn I hit a patch of gravel in the road and my bike and I went down. I tried to get up, but I was told by the people who'd been riding behind me that my bike had flipped into the air and slammed down on my back, so I was probably busted up pretty good inside.

As God would have it there were a few paramedics riding with us who kept me calm and stable until the ambulance arrived, which was only a couple of minutes since I went down not more than a mile or two from a paramedic sub-station. Isn't God good! Twice in the ambulance, they almost lost me; my blood pressure bottomed out and they were able to get it back up just in time. When I got to the hospital, which had one of the top 100 trauma centers in the country, they almost lost me again in the Emergency Room. My attending nurse was the wife of a pastor, and the surgeon assigned to me was also a Christian. God is really amazing, isn't He? All together, I had a collapsed lung, a bruised kidney, a ruptured spleen, and three broken ribs—a pretty good amount of damage.

64

I stayed in the hospital for twelve days, and then traveled home. Apparently the ride home finished off what damage there was to my spleen. The next day I almost died in my youngest son's arms from internal bleeding while waiting for the ambulance to arrive, which only took about two minutes because they were in the area (what a surprise). I had emergency surgery to remove my spleen and basically had to have my entire blood supply replaced.

If God had not placed everyone where He did through this whole experience, I would have died at any of the five or six critical moments. I believe Satan tried to take me out before I could gain any momentum in the motorcycle ministry. Instead, God has renewed my spirit as well as my body and we are starting to make major advances into the enemy camp: one hardcore biker saved so far, several seeking answers, and it has galvanized my small group of warriors into a spiritual SWAT team with full armor on and swords in hand. I thank God every day for that "accident," and for what it has done for me spiritually, in my family, and in my ministry. Also, I'm thankful for the diligence and fellowship from Messiah's Messengers of Charlestown, VA for without them my ministry, as well as my life, would not be going strong today.

A Matter of Life or Death

David Adams, Minnesota, CMA No. 61,298

My first encounter with CMA was in February 1996, and as I think back to where I was when I discovered this ministry I am reminded that God is still in the miracle business. In the fall of that year, we had lived in the Chicago area for four years, following our fourth cross-country move since I had accepted Jesus as my Lord and Savior in 1979. Each move meant the painful experience of pulling up of roots and moving on. Landing in the Chicago area, I concluded it would be less painful if I didn't put roots down in the first place. The only problem with that philosophy is that one tends to get bounced around by every blowing wind, and by that fall, I was being blown around a lot, picking up some painful bruises in the process.

One Saturday, while walking behind a mower in bad need of a new muffler, I began looking to my past for answers, because all I was finding looking forward were more questions, darkness, and despair. I thought back to the 1960s when I participated at my father's side in the blue-collar politics of northern Idaho's mining and logging country. The memories of the campaigns returned and put a smile on my face, something I had not had in awhile. The pressing of the flesh, sharing with others about things I felt strongly about, and traveling to different towns and political rallies had gotten into my blood. Tracing back over the aimless path of my life, I asked myself, 'How did I end up in Chicago, when all I wanted to do was stay in Idaho where I knew and understood the politics, the people, and the land?' Then it hit me, Chicago! I was located in one of the most "A" political areas in the country and the answer was obvious; it was time to get involved again.

On the next pass of the mower my thinking hit an abrupt stop when a question came from what I call "that silent voice within," the voice of the Holy Spirit, never audible, but always unmistakable. "Would you campaign for Me?" He asked. There was no question as to who the "Me" was.

I stopped and shut the noisy mower off and thought for a second. 'Whoa, what do I do with that?' If I said yes, I didn't have a clue how to go about campaigning for Jesus Christ. If I said no the next questions were obvious, "Why, are you ashamed of Me? Is there something better about the politicians?" All I could say was, "Yes Lord, I will, but You're going to have to show me how, because I don't have a clue what to do." With that, the voice went quiet. I wishfully thought that perhaps God was just testing me to see how I would react, but I knew deep inside this was not going to be the end of it.

In the months that followed, I slid deeper into a dark abyss, which was not new to me having struggled with chronic depression for years. One January day in 1997, while standing on a cold elevated train platform in Chicago's Loop, I concluded it was time to get off the rollercoaster ride of ups and downs. There was a concrete abutment on a rural road a few miles south of our house and hitting it at a high speed with my 550cc street bike would be the final and ultimate solution to the problems and failures I faced throughout my life. No one would suspect a suicide. I would be just another person who lost control of his motorcycle.

It did not take my wife, Mary Ann, long to figure out where my mind was going, and she pressed hard for me to get help. This led me to a Christian counseling service and a referral to a psychiatrist. They put me on anti-depressants and advised me to get involved in church or something similar.

As I thought about what and where, I recalled a motorcycle swap meet I had gone to in February the year before and the Christian biker booth there. I dug through an old pile of stuff I had accumulated, located the phone number, and got information about their Sunday ride and meetings. I showed up for the ride and found a group of people who didn't push religion on me. They accepted me as another rider. It was unlike any other encounters I had had with churches or Christian groups.

A few weeks later I joined them for their Run for the Son ride and May meeting where I learned about a bike blessing they were conducting for a group. I put my name on the list of those who would help out; mostly to see what would happen and thinking it should be interesting.

I had been showing up for this group's events for less than a month, but you would have thought I had been with the chapter since its founding. I assumed the man in charge of the bike blessing was going to do the prayer over all the bikes, but when he gave us instructions, it dawned on me this was a one on one event.

"Introduce yourself, ask their name, and if they want their bike blessed. Then pray over the bike, move close to them, and incorporate their name in the prayer; pray boldly," he advised us.

The group of bikers rolling in for the event looked as though they hadn't been to church since their mothers gave up dragging them there at about age 5. After watching the CMAers pray with some of the riders, I figured the worst thing that could happen is they would say no. I approached a biker who rode up on what would win any rat bike contest hands down. I introduced myself as he responded in kind. We shook hands and talked about his bike that he was rather proud of having built it from the ground up himself using parts from everything imaginable.

"Would you like the bike blessed, John?" I asked.

He looked at the bike and with a humorous grin on his face, shrugged, "Yeah, why not!"

To both our surprise I took his hand in mine, grabbed hold of the handlebars, and prayed for John's bike then incorporated John by name asking that his heart would be open to God during the riding season, and that he would experience Jesus' unconditional love for him. When I finished, John's expression changed from humorous to sincere appreciation. As he looked me in the eyes, he said, "Thanks," shook my hand, and moved on to register for the event.

I prayed with many others that day and after watching the bikes roll out on the run, I walked back to my new bike with no more than 10 miles on the odometer that I had just taken delivery of the day before. I was on an emotional high similar to those I experienced when I campaigned with my dad. Then, once again that silent voice within spoke, "David, you just campaigned for Me." I had pressed the flesh and I had shared something I strongly believed in. All the elements of what I loved about political campaigns were there. Within the month, I ordered the Ministry Team tapes. As I listened to them, a fire grew in my heart for the CMA ministry.

As I look over the past eleven years since the Lord asked me if I would campaign for Jesus, I see nothing less than a miracle in my involvement in CMA. Through CMA, my motorcycle transformed from a machine that was to have been an instrument of my life-ending self-destruction, to a tool to reach others with the lifesaving message of the gospel. CMA became a lifesaving experience.

That new bike that had 10 miles on it at that first bike blessing has rolled over 87,000 miles since then. I am campaigning for Jesus, a campaign that will only end on the ultimate day of decision. It is the most important campaign I have ever been involved with because it is nothing less than a matter of life or death for those we reach out to.

Ask Me About the Day I Died

Tim Newland, Texas, CMA No. 90,673

It was about 7:30 a.m. on a Saturday morning, April Fools Day, when the phone rang. Alice and I were still lying in bed. It was Mark Broberg calling about a motorcycle we had been talking about the week before. We talked for a while and after we hung up, I told Alice I wasn't feeling well. She said we had nothing planned and we could just rest a while. I suddenly got nauseated and went to the bathroom and threw up really hard. I have not done that since my drinking days over twenty years ago. I came back to bed and it felt like an elephant placed his big wide foot on my chest, but not bearing down real hard. I got nauseated again and went to the bathroom again with a repeat performance, except I got diarrhea at the same time. I made it back to bed again and then it felt like the elephant pressed all his weight on me. I told Alice I needed to go the hospital—quick.

I have had two heart attacks with over 15 angioplasties, so we knew the drill well. I got nauseated again, and while I was in the bathroom I remembered what they had told me several years ago at Cooper's Aerobics Center during heart rehab. They said most fatal heart attacks happen in the morning and the victims are found in the toilet throwing up. I made it back to bed with that elephant bearing down full force on my chest. The pain was intense and it felt like he was pressing all of the fluid out of my chest and into my arms and neck. I knew this was serious, as I could not get my breath, and every breath felt like the last; characteristics of a bad heart attack.

I told Alice to call 911; I didn't have time for her to take me to Presbyterian Hospital in Dallas. EMS was there quickly and they saw how bad I was. They said they didn't have time to take me to Presbyterian and said they would take me to Garland Baylor, the closest heart trauma hospital. I felt a sense of doom as they put me on a hard stretcher and wheeled me out to the ambulance. One guy drove the ambulance and the other rode in the back with me.

As they were loading me, I saw Alice, and I had the strange feeling I would never see her again. Though I was not afraid of dying, the thought of not seeing her again made me start to panic and realize how serious this really was. Then the ambulance sped off. In the midst of all the excitement, they had forgotten to strap me down to the stretcher and with the slick material of my jogging suit, I propelled into the back doors of the ambulance. The guy with me did not notice. I was just praying that the back doors were locked or I would end up in the street. I almost came completely off the stretcher when they had to make a turn. When the driver hit his brakes, I came back the other way as fast as I did backwards. Then he pressed the gas again and I went back into the doors. This happened about three times before the guy in the back could get me strapped down. It was as if I was outside my body watching this on TV's Funniest Videos. I forgot all about what was going on and started laughing, almost giggling at what was happening. Most people in that situation would have gotten mad, but I know now it was God doing something to get my mind off what was happening. God has a sense of humor in the midst of tragedy; He knew exactly what I needed at that very moment.

We pulled into the hospital and I saw the red lights bouncing off the walls as the door opened. The pain now was more than I could bear. I remember a lot of chaotic things happening all around me. The sounds were loud, fast, and frantic. I knew I was the center of attention by many people doing many things. Then all that ended and I was in a very calm and very safe place. The best I can explain it is the feeling a baby must feel when you wrap it in a swaddling blanket and hold it close to your chest. I felt peace and it felt like it was forever. I didn't see bright lights or loud voices, but I knew I was in the presence of something very special. Like I said, I didn't hear voices, but I understood what was being said to me, "I am proud of you; you have been obedient and have done everything I have asked of you. You can come with me now or you can stay, it's your choice." I wanted to go with Him and be free from the intense pain I was experiencing, but then I thought about Alice and the new grandbabies, my sister and her kids. He told me, "Don't worry about them, I will take care of them." I knew then I would be leaving with Him in my next breath. Then I saw a small valley with a hill in the background. There were thousands of people and each one was pleading with me to stay, saying, "You promised me; you promised me." What had I promised them? Who were these people? I knew there was more to this than I comprehended. What should I do? I knew I couldn't go now.

After they wheeled me into the hospital, I don't remember anything for the next four days, except for two things. One was when they had ice all over me with a fan and I was freezing and my body was shaking. Later I found out that I'd had a fever they were trying to control. The next was Harvey Keil, a fellow CMAer being next to my bed talking about RFS. I am sure he prayed for me as well (that is Harvey's nature), but I don't remember it. While he was talking about RFS, I saw those people again in the valley and on the hill saying, "You promised; you promised; you're going to make it." What had I promised to so many people that meant so much? Then John McDowell came to mind and I remembered talking with him several years ago, when he and Wendy raised so much money for RFS. He told me it was not for ego or recognition; instead, it was because he knew for every dollar he raised, a soul would be added to God's Kingdom. Then it all started coming together. I remembered that I wrote down a pledge at a monthly chapter meeting with the amount of money Alice and I were going to give to RFS. These were all the people I would have sold out if I didn't give the money I promised. I knew I had to make it through all this to do it.

When I started remembering and realized where I was and what was happening to me, I knew I was going to make it. I had no doubt because I knew I had to fulfill the promise I had made and God was going to give me the strength and power to do just that.

I couldn't wait to get to the next chapter meeting to turn in our donation. The doctors told me I would never ride my scooter again and not knowing what to expect in the near future, I wanted to turn the donation in as soon as I could. Believe me, Satan fought me all the way to that gathering that night, and a couple times I didn't think I was going to make it. I could hardly walk without losing my breath. I didn't know if I should even be driving the car. Alice couldn't come with me to drive because our daughter had hurt herself and she had to take care of the grandbaby. Satan lost the fight that night and those people will get their place in heaven. I can't tell you how wonderful I felt handing my RFS envelope to our secretary, Vicky Coleman, that night. What a deal: a dollar for a soul–there is no better deal anywhere.

I am very proud of our chapter. Over the past years we have raised almost $300,000 which is 300,000 souls–the size of a pretty large city. In four of the past five years, our chapter, Faith Riders, has been the number one chapter for RFS donations. We have been labeled as the rich North Dallas Chapter, but that is not the case. The truth is we all understand the eternal significance for RFS and will do everything we can to bring lost souls into the hands of our Heavenly Father. We take RFS very seriously.

Does it take a heart attack to see what RFS is all about? I hope not. But it sure opened my eyes and heart to the true mission.

One week after that chapter meeting, I went into cardiac arrest from the heart damage suffered only weeks before, and fell dead on a McDonald's parking lot. Luckily I was with my chapter and they laid hands on me and prayed over me. The next thing I remember was a voice saying, "Jesus…please don't let him die." They rushed me to the hospital, again in an ambulance. The doctors told Alice and me it was a miracle that I came back–only 1% of the people who go into cardiac arrest come back to life without electrical shock. Three days later they put a defibrillator in my chest and told me I would never ride my motorcycle again and my life would never be the same. I drove my car to the CMA National Rally in Hatfield, AR a couple of months later. After one of the services, I asked Curtis Clements to pray over me that I would be healed and that I would ride my scooter again. By the grace of God, my defibrillator has never gone off and I was able to ride my scooter to the Changing of the Colors in October, leading two rides cross the mountains. Praise God!

I would be in heaven today if it were not for the thousands of men, women, and children that God showed me on that hillside saying, "Please don't go; you promised." And by the way, I didn't expect it, but at the CMA National Rally that year, I was honored as being the 10th highest individual contributor to RFS. The biggest honor, however, is when I'll get to meet all those people in Heaven. What a day of rejoicing that will be!

I now wear a pin on my vest that says, "Ask me about the day I died." This is the story I tell.

Thank you, CMA, for sponsoring Run for the Son and for my brothers and sisters of Faith Riders in Plano, Texas. God is very pleased with what you do. And a special thanks to my wife, Alice, who supports me when God calls me to His service, no matter how crazy it may seem.

They Made a Run for the Son *Walk* in Prison

Harlan Powell, Arkansas, CMA No. 62,683

A former prisoner named Mark told the following story about a group of men who did an RFS *walk* in a prison at Mount Pleasant, Iowa, in 2001:

Mark and a friend named Gary, both inmates at the prison, got together with some other inmates (also CMAers), and planned an RFS project.

Since prison rules didn't allow the inmates to receive donations, the guys contacted the CMA chapter in Ottumwa, Iowa, to ask them to help by collecting the donations. The inmates wrote to friends and relatives asking them to support the effort. They were thrilled to see the response was favorable.

The plan was to walk laps around the quarter-mile prison yard perimeter. Mark agreed to walk ten miles, in spite of the fact he had suffered five heart attacks prior to his confinement. Others agreed to walk with them...some more miles, some less. Mark's friend Gary announced he wanted to walk the whole one hundred miles (the normal RFS distance). That would be 400 laps! Just for Gary!

There were two separate yards in the compound, and two weeks before the planned RFS walk, prison officials made changes as to which yard different pods would go to for their time of outdoor recreation. Mark exclaimed, "Wouldn't you know it!" Most of the CMAers wound up in the same yard. Thank you, Jesus."

But not everything would go so well. On Friday, the day before the walk, Gary woke up with a huge swollen ankle. He hadn't twisted it or tripped, so it was obviously an attack from Satan. On Saturday morning, Gary's ankle was still swollen so it was agreed by all that he shouldn't walk.

That small band of CMA inmates got together and worked out a deal. They would divide up Gary's hundred miles and walk them for him. Mark added five miles to his ten, but within that small group, there still weren't enough guys to walk all of Gary's miles. Word about anything spreads like wildfire in prison. In this case, it was the news about Gary's swollen ankle and his foiled plan to walk a hundred miles for CMA's annual fundraiser for world missions.

When the cell blocks started emptying out, the "brothers in blue" (fellow inmates) started going to Gary where he was perched to count the laps. Many inmates came to help, both the saved and the lost. When Gary totaled up the miles his fellow inmates walked for him that Saturday, it was well over three hundred miles—twelve hundred laps in all!

Mark managed to raise about $75 for his part in that run, but the group as a whole raised a little over $500, according to a report from the chapter in Ottumwa. Mark believes this was the first time a prison CMA fellowship (though unchartered and unofficial) actually carried out a Run for the Son. In this case, they walked their miles on a prison yard instead of riding them on a highway.

Giving What You Have Unto the Lord

Rhea Ward, Georgia, CMA No. 95,933

In July 2002, my neighbor, Edith Pierce, contacted me about getting our bluegrass gospel group to play at her church. Edith had ridden motorcycles and been in CMA for several years, and I would see her ride by my house all the time. She shared with me about the ministry of CMA, including RFS. I thought it was cool how she rode a motorcycle for Jesus. She and I became good friends.

I got excited about CMA and especially about the RFS donations of motorcycles to missionaries. Soon I began to share with my business clients and friends about RFS and CMA. Then, I started praying for the local chapter.

In February 2003, Edith invited me to attend the HOG Bike Show at a local mall–it hooked me! I liked all the motorcycles and especially the black leather clothes that the motorcyclists wore. But the fact that CMA was out there "where the rubber meets the road" trying to win folks to Christ really hit me and I wanted to be a part of it all.

In March, with the help of my dad, I picked out and purchased my first Harley Davidson. It was a red 1998 883 Sportster. Within two days of bringing it home, the bike and I went through the ditch in front of my house. I didn't have any broken bones, but what pain from the bruises! I got my "crash" course out of the way right quick.

This woke me up as to what can happen on a motorcycle. I took a few months to heal and then I purchased a Honda Rebel 250, as the Harley was too much bike to learn on. I had never ridden anything but a Honda 100 in the field beside my house and I had never ridden on the road before.

My friends, Edith Pierce and Myrtice Shepherd, began to work with me to teach me to ride safely. Edith started me off in the living room on a chair. Then she got me to riding up and down my short, paved driveway. Eventually both ladies and my dad took me to a large parking lot to practice my riding. Next I completed a motorcycle safety class and studied and got my learner's license. Finally, they took me on my first road trip. Edith and Myrtice rode in front of me, with my Dad following in the truck. We drove fifteen miles that day at only 25 to 30 miles per hour.

For the next six months, I rode my little Honda Rebel over 3,000 miles. Often I would be out riding–just "me and Jesus." I would sing and pray as I rode. I will never forget one day when I was out riding, Jesus spoke to me in a voice I could hear. He said, "This has gotten much bigger than learning to ride a motorcycle so you can ride with Edith. Will you ride for ME?" And I said, "Yes, Lord, I'll ride for You." The wind blew the tears back from my eyes as I rode.

In January 2004, I got back on the Sportster and began to ride it on the road. I got my full motorcycle license a few months later and I began to ride the Sportster full-time.

During this time, I was inspired to raise money for RFS. I told my clients about RFS, and collected donations. I also went to a few local churches to speak, play my banjo, and show the RFS video. The Lord helped me to raise over $1,550 that year.

The Lord asked me to make a CD with my then 82-year-old mother. We laid all the tracks: I played the 5-string banjo, guitar, bass, fiddle, and sang; my mother played piano and sang. We called our first CD the *Mom and Daughter* album. I prayed for the Lord to open doors for me to use my talents for Him in CMA and other ways. Little did I know what lay ahead!

I laid my life on the altar and prayed that I would go wherever He wanted me to go and do whatever He wanted me to do. Watch out when you get to praying like that!

In August of 2004, I attended the CMA Georgia State Rally where Mr. John Ogden, Sr., CMA Chairman of the Board, was a guest speaker. He liked my banjo playing so much he invited me to play at the CMA Changing of the Colors Rally in Hatfield, Arkansas. In October, Mike & JoAnn Cook hauled my Sportster in the back of their truck and I followed in my car.

While playing at the rally we collected donations for RFS from the sale of *Mom and Daughter* CDs and were able to raise $4,203. I was the third highest RFS fundraiser in the state of Georgia.

In 2005, I played at the Changing of the Colors Rally, again. We did a second CD, *Mom and Daughter-Volume 2*, and with the Lord's help raised $5,130 for RFS. I was the third highest RFS fundraiser in the state of Georgia, again.

It was at the 2004 Changing of the Colors Rally that I met my husband-to-be, Russ Ward, from Omaha, Nebraska. The Lord brought us together and after a long-distance courtship and lots of prayer, we were married on May 20, 2006, in Macon, Georgia. We repeated our vows in Council Bluffs, Iowa, on May 28, 2006.

For our Georgia wedding we had a bluegrass, motorcycle, traditional wedding. Edith was my matron of honor and my fellow chapter members were my bridesmaids and grooms-men. Both my chapter and another nearby chapter were there and helped in many ways. Over half of the wedding was bluegrass gospel music with a gospel presentation and invitation prior to the ceremony. We left in our leathers on Russ's Heritage Softail Classic.

Wow! Praise the Lord! Run for the Son and CMA have really changed my life and I am so grateful to the Lord for bringing this ministry into my life. The Lord has brought me from a homebody who had done mainly ministry in the church and who traveled only locally to someone traveling on a motorcycle all over the United States sharing the gospel in music and song. In October of 2006, Edith accompanied me on guitar as I played for the Changing of the Colors Rally for the third time.

My next ministry project is to record a third CD, with Edith on guitar and me on banjo, to raise more money for RFS. Russ and I plan to buy a motorcycle trailer to carry the banjo so that we may travel and share music with other CMA and motorcycle rallies around the United States.

What About the Other 40%?

Harlan Powell, Arkansas, CMA No. 62,683

Have you ever wondered what kind of returns we get from the portion of RFS money that is spent on evangelism here in the United States?

The annual Blowout on the Mississippi Gulf Coast is one of the bigger motorcycle rallies in the United States, a rough and rowdy event that's always held on Memorial Day weekend. A well known local club manages and controls the rally, and many 1%ers of various brotherhoods ride in to join the non-stop partying. It seems that just as many bankers, account-ants, and other career people who ride motorcycles, are lured in each year by the stories they hear.

Prior to my first ride to the Blowout some years back, our chapter president cautioned us that this event was not for everyone. As mentioned above, it is rough and rowdy. Still, he told us, it is a field very ripe for ministry.

So, inside the grounds of the racetrack where the event is held, my first time there, I stayed close to the CMA hospitality table. The constant roar of motorcycles on the move and the noise of people up partying all around made sleep difficult, and I found myself sitting at the CMA tent even at night. And the coffee, available to me as well as to those bleary-eyed night owls who came to our tent, never ran out.

I went back to the Blowout the following year, but it wasn't until my third year there that I noticed the vast quantities of cups, rags, and tracts that were required to work such a big rally. It was obvious the nearby chapters, or even the state as a whole, could not bear the cost of ministry materials needed for such a large event.

Our RFS flyers and letters state that 60% of the money raised goes to three ministries doing worldwide evangelism, and most great testimonies seem to come from them, but what about the other 40%? Well, that's how we manage to carry big quantities of cups, rags, and tracts to rallies like the Blowout. I witnessed, at that Sunday morning service beside the race-track, my third visit to the Blowout, what the testimonies can be.

A CMAer with a guitar got up to sing and open the service. A larger than usual crowd of bikers sat in the bleachers. The cups, rags, and tracts had done their prep work. After a couple of songs, the singer paused and started talking.

"You know, I was 38 years old when I quit running from God and I got saved. And, now, looking back, it's a mystery to me why I ever ran from God in the first place. God says it would be wrong for me to steal another man's motorcycle, or to run off with another man's wife. I can't argue with God about those matters. God is right, and I agree with Him. So why was I running? Some of you guys sitting there have codes of honor and conduct in your clubs. So, let me ask you, can you argue with God about what He says is right and what He says is wrong?"

After one more song, the singer moved quietly from the microphone and the evangelist came on to speak his message. He said he had a prepared message, but he took what the singer had started about choosing to obey God or choosing to disobey Him and built his brief message on that.

When the evangelist closed with a simple prayer and invitation, more than 25 hands went up to join in the sinner's prayer for salvation. **More than a few of those who accepted salvation that day wore 1% patches.**

There are probably hundreds—make that thousands—of stories about what our 40% of the RFS money is doing here at home. This has been just one of them.

Run for the Son Encourages All Believers

Chari "Coach" Bouse, Texas, CMA No. 76,566

Just before RFS in May of 2005, I had to make an unexpected trip to see my OB/GYN. Though not an emergency, it was close, especially since I was nearing my "year of Jubilee." I had not seen this doctor for over five years, as he was not on our new PPO plan. However, the thought of going to a new doctor that was on our plan was not comforting at all. After a little prayer, I felt peace about going back to my old doctor, even if it meant paying more money–there are some things a gal just can't compromise.

The morning of the exam came and I was preparing to leave when I felt a prodding from the Holy Spirit to take a CMA *Hope for the Highway* Bible. Next to it were RFS brochures, so I stuck one inside the Bible.

After I filled out a mountain of paperwork, the nurse showed me to an exam room and asked me to put on one of the lovely pink gowns. (I don't think they get those from Macy's). I changed and just before sitting on the exam table I put the Bible and RFS brochure on the little desk by the doctor's chair. A few moments later, the doctor entered the room with a forced smile on his face. He seemed happy to see me, but I could tell something was really bothering him. After we shook hands, he turned and saw the items on his desk. He picked up the Bible with a shocked look on his face. "Tell me about this," he said as he plopped down in his chair. After I finished explaining everything to him, his eyes were full of tears.

He then shared that he was a Christian (I never knew this before) and had just bought a Harley Heritage Softail. He had been asking, "God, why did you want me to buy this motorcycle?" and then I showed up with CMA materials. He had never heard of CMA or RFS. He said he'd been in such a funk lately that he was planning to cancel his annual medical mission trip

82

to Central America. For the next forty-five minutes (while freezing in my drafty pink gown), I ministered to this doctor about *changing the world, one heart at a time* like CMA does, and not trying to take on a whole country. Finally his nurse came in and asked, "Are you going to examine this patient today?" When he stood up he was a different man. He was smiling and thanking God for sending him information about CMA and the great things they do.

The impact RFS has on the world goes way beyond those in other lands who receive funds, supplies, motorcycles, and Bibles. Just the great testimonies of past RFS runs were enough encouragement for this doctor to come out of depression and realize his work was just as important...if he approached it *one heart at a time*. He is now back to his ministry of medical missions and, of course, he still has his Harley.

Oh, and the problem that made me go to him in the first place? It miraculously went away after that visit–just another divine appointment in disguise.

A God Thing

Gordon Wyrick, Texas, CMA No. 27,118

Just before the 2001 RFS, I was in my pickup heading to a benefit at a biker bar on I-45 when I saw two bikers on the side of the road with bikes that appeared to be broken down. I don't stop every time I see bikers on the side of the road, but this time something caused me to turn around (a God thing) to see if I could help. The two bikers seemed grateful that someone would stop. One of the guys then decided to walk back to the bar they had just left to get some help.

The biker who remained with the bikes noticed my CMA colors and started asking about CMA. I shared what CMA was all about and told him about RFS. This biker owned his own business which was doing very well financially. I'm not sure whether he knew the Lord, but I knew he had a giving heart because he was already sending money to a mission in South America. He asked how he could help CMA. I told him more about RFS and left some literature and my business card with him.

His friend showed up and we chatted for awhile. When I left those guys, I didn't know whether I would ever see or hear from them again. A few days later, there was an envelope in the mail from a business I didn't recognize. I opened the envelope and to my surprise there was a check for $1,000, made out to CMA for RFS. It came from the biker I had shared with on the side of the road. What I learned was that I just have to be available and let God do the work.

All God wants from us is to be ready to give a reason for the hope within us and to share His Love. Only He can move and change men's hearts.

Wholeness Found in Christ

Thomas Barber, Texas, CMA No. 95,114

Having been a Christian and serving in the church in several areas, I knew God was using that time for His glory. However, I felt a deep need to do more for God, but had no clue how to go about it. A friend of mine kept trying to get me to go to a CMA meeting with him to see what serving Christ with a motorcycle was about. I finally gave in and went. This is where I found a way to step up how to serve, witness, and share about God's glory. I found my niche and began studying the ministry tapes. I fought with God as He kept telling me to do the Prison Ministry Team. Finally, I followed God in faith and went through the series. The team tapes opened my eyes on how to earn the right and respect of others, while setting a path that led to sharing Christ with the lost. It placed methods, opportunities, and divine appointments into a perspective I have never seen.

The strongest time in a ministry opportunity I have had was at a youth facility. As we went in, I prayed, "Lord, guide me to which door you want me to step through, I will go." He led me to a 14-year-old girl that had experienced the exact things that had plagued me as a child–abuse in too many ways to share. I knew God had prepared me to share with her. We spoke and I shared from the *Hope for the Highway* Bible (which I left with her). I listened, asked questions, and prayed with her. At one point, I saw tears running down her face. I asked what had made her cry, and she stated that she had never met anyone before that so closely shared the horrible experiences of her life that had made it the other end of the tunnel, meaning reaching a point where I could fully turn my life over to God and let Him heal me.

Had it not been for the training CMA provided and the materials they produced I probably would have never considered going into a prison to share the gospel. However, God used

85

my love for motorcycles to draw me closer to Him, and CMA had the materials to teach me how to serve in ways I had never considered.

Through listening to the tapes, I also used the acronym of L-O-S-T when speaking to a member of a very rough biker club. Having an understanding of how to open the door, I met and talked with the person and later had an opportunity to assist him and his wife in keeping the electricity and gas on in their home in the middle of a very cold winter. As time went on we were able to continue to minister to this couple using the *Hope for the Highway* Bible and we witnessed a change in his heart. He laid down his colors, left the club, started going to church, and even calls us when he needs prayer. In addition, he has spoken to prospects about another path. This is all after his 30 years of loyalty to this club. His wife has published a book about how the CMA chapter changes lives through their testimony of Jesus.

This is an example of how CMA has touched four lives–mine by equipping me to serve God and take the gospel into the community. Three by using the tools in CMA's toolkit and the experiences of my past to reach the hearts of these three people, showing them that giving their hearts to God and having faith in His Word will change them forever.

Comfort in the Face of Trials

Carol Jones, Colorado, CMA No. 104,729

My husband, Bruce, and I were barely making it in our marriage. We were living in separate worlds in the same house, but then an amazing God-thing happened; we joined CMA. We fell in love with the way our chapter loved God and us, it was that love that brought us back for more and drew us together as a couple. Our weeks were filled with events and the anticipation of seeing our CMA family was electrifying. My husband and I were doing things together, helping and serving others and that began to bring us closer as a couple. CMA has changed our lives, marriage, and future.

In 2005, we found ourselves in Sturgis, and because I am a nurse, I volunteered at the Rapid City Hospital. Bruce, anxious about the thought of volunteering as a hospital chaplain, found himself in a very unfamiliar setting. Everyday we had the opportunity to enter a hospital room and pray for the needs of a fallen biker. We experienced closeness and a bond as we walked the halls of the hospital.

One afternoon, shortly after arriving, I saw a sight all too familiar–a down biker was being rushed from the flight-for-life helicopter into the Emergency Room (ER). The ER staff ushered me back to be part of what turned into a life-changing experience.

The transport team and I arrived in the ER at the same time, along with three young men who were barely able to compose themselves. There on the table lay a 30-year-old man who choose that day not to wear his helmet, took a curve at about 50 miles an hour, and went down. His head and the pavement met with a tragic blow. He had a severe head injury, major abrasions, and open wounds. I introduced myself, and I attempted to comfort his friends. When I offered to pray, they told me they were believers and that began a wonderful bond with these three friends and CMA.

Bruce assessed the situation and reported what was happening to the CMA chaplain. Within minutes, there was help from the CMA family. They had someone on standby to transport the family from the airport to the hospital, bring meals to the grieving friends and family, and assist with picking up and transporting the wrecked bike back to Minnesota. Their tireless support left me in awe.

The director of the ICU asked if I would go in with the wife and offer support, I did. I knew God had put a team of angels there that day to bless a fallen brother, his family, and his friends. The decision was made to take him off life-support and once again, CMA was asked by the hospital staff to be there for the family, we were and this loved brother/husband/father went home to be with the Lord. I had no idea the depth of support and love that we are a part of, but that day I realized CMA is more than just an organization, it is God in the flesh, doing whatever it takes to touch lives.

Divine Appointment

Denny White, New York, CMA No. 117,728

On our way home from the 2006 Daytona Bike Week, my friends and I stopped at a rest area off Interstate 95 in Florida. I saw that the Christian Motorcyclists Association had set up an information booth there, and were offering bottles of water. When I attempted to pay for one, the couple at the booth told me the water was free. I made a donation and began to look at the literature on display. The woman told me to help myself to anything I wanted; the one thing that caught my eye was a miniature Bible called *Hope for the Highway*. In the past, I had thought about reading the Bible, but had not ever made the effort, so I took a copy. When I got home I set it down on a table, and there it stayed for several weeks.

One evening early in April 2006, I was pulled over and arrested for driving while intoxicated, or DWI. To complicate matters, I had another DWI conviction on my record from 9 years ago, making this my second DWI within ten years, making it a felony conviction. The next morning, which just happened to be Palm Sunday, I found myself in a deep, dark state of depression. I had hit rock bottom! I did not have any idea who to turn to or how to cope with what had happened. Later that day, I headed to church.

Since it was mid-afternoon, the church was completely empty. I begged God for His forgiveness and asked Him for His guidance. I left the church about an hour later feeling like a new person, enjoying indescribable feelings of peace and confidence, knowing God would answer my prayers and help me turn this negative time in my life into a positive opportunity to serve Him.

In addition to saying my regular prayers, I committed to reading the Bible daily. Within a few weeks, I was hooked. The *Hope for the Highway* Bible and the testimonies it contained inspired me to call the CMA National phone number listed in the back. First, I wanted to thank them for the Bible and tell them how it helped change my life. Second, I wanted to find out what CMA was all about and what it represented.

They referred me to CMA's New York State Coordinator, Kurt Repsher, and when I called him, we spoke for nearly 2 hours. The more I heard the more I wanted to know about God, and also how to become part of CMA. During our conversation, Kurt told me about a prayer for salvation. As I prayed with him, I felt my heart was being changed forever. Kurt referred me to Mike Canny, who was the acting president of a new forming chapter near my home.

When I called Mike to introduce myself, I told him how God had led me on this journey to CMA, and then he shared a few similar setbacks that he had experienced in his life over the years. Our conversation helped mend my bruised self-esteem, and I knew immediately I wanted to become a member of the local CMA chapter. I am proud to say the chapter recently elected me as road captain, and we received our official charter at New York's 2007 Seasons of Refreshing!

Sometimes it is hard for me to process the fact that so much has happened in my life in less than a year—so much has radically changed for the better. I always thought I had strong faith, but I never knew it was possible to have the personal relationship with our Lord that I enjoy now.

In closing, I am thankful for CMA—they're really making a difference in people's lives, and I am living proof. I feel truly blessed to be a part of the CMA family. Who would have thought that a simple rest area stop to get water could lead to eternal salvation?!

SECTION FIVE:

Foreign Missions

Lord, I'll Go! Send Me.

Renea Harris, RN, Florida, CMA No. 67,751

In 2001, my husband, David, and I attended the CMA Florida State Rally. At the rally, Gary announced that there was an upcoming CMA mission trip to Peru. David whispered to me that we ought to go. Monday morning I called CMA headquarters only to be told the team was full and we would be put on a waiting list. David was relieved when I told him this as he didn't remember saying we should go. I prayed and prayed that we would be accepted.

After a few anxious weeks, we received the call I had prayed for. In October of 2001, David and I, along with several other CMAers, went to Peru. We traveled to a number of ministry points during our trip. One of my favorite memories of the trip was the sight of my husband, the reluctant missionary, playing games with the children, acting like a child, and holding babies with no fear of getting wet upon. He really engaged with the children of Peru.

I assisted in a feeding program for the children. I was asked to ladle out boiling hot chocolate that had been cooked in a large pot that sat on top of logs placed in the corner of a church with a dirt floor. What they called hot chocolate didn't smell nor look like hot chocolate to me. The children lined up holding their little chipped tin cups. I was filling the cups only half-full since the liquid was boiling hot. The pastor's wife saw what I was doing and told me to fill the cups all the way to the top and not to worry about them burning their hands, as their hands were extremely calloused and this was a special treat for them. My heart broke and the tears flowed.

We were thrilled to be part of a bike presentation in Puerto Maldonado to Pastor David. I was surprised at the large number of people who were at the meeting as this was a special service just for the bike presentation. Our team gave Pastor David a helmet, a CMA sticker for his bike, and a backpack to carry his Bible. After the presentation, one by one the congregation came up to each of us and either gave us a handshake or a hug and kiss. When I thought all the members had thanked us I looked up and saw an elderly lady, who was extremely bent over, walking with a cane trying to make her way up to the platform where we were. She hugged each of us and thanked us for giving her pastor the bike. This RFS bike meant she was going to get to see her pastor much more often, so the bike was just as much a gift to her as it was to him.

Another memory that we came away from this trip with was when several of the team members were not feeling well due to the high altitude in the mountains of Peru. When we traveled to a village, those who were feeling sick stayed on the bus while the rest of us went to visit the people. The villagers wanted to honor the team so they slaughtered a lamb and cooked it over an open fire. They placed the whole lamb in a burlap-type sack, and carried it, with feet sticking up in the air, onto the bus. They had full intentions of serving it to the team right there on the bus. Luckily before they made their first swing with the machete they were guided off the bus and back to a local home where the lamb was served along with potatoes and bread to those team members who were not ill. What a sacrifice this was for them; I felt so unworthy.

Over the years since that trip I have followed Pastor David's activities. His congregation has grown and he has started a home for unwed mothers. The home takes the mother and the baby, and cares for the baby until it turns eighteen years of age. The mothers are taught skills to support themselves and are also taught the gospel. The local politicians were so impressed with Pastor David's integrity and what he was doing with these girls that they offered him a plot of land to build the first Christian School in Puerto Maldonado.

The following year I went on a trip to Haiti with an MVI medical team. Being honest, I must admit that I didn't go out of compassion, but out of curiosity. After being in Peru and seeing the living conditions, I just couldn't imagine how a medical clinic could be set up in such an environment. While in Haiti, I held a two-year-old girl who was dying of AIDS–she weighed only ten pounds. The empty look in her eyes and the look of despair in her mother's eyes were haunting. That night when I went to bed I thought of this child; my heart broke. Throughout the night I kept hearing the words, "Ye who have so little faith, trust in Me and doors will open." When morning came I knew what I had to do. I called my husband David and asked if I could come home and resign from my job to volunteer with MVI to organize their medical mission teams. At the time I was earning 60% of our household income, but David lovingly said, "You know I will support you in whatever you want to do."

This was three-and-a-half years ago. Since then I have gone on over twenty mission trips around the world. I have also had the pleasure of working with Gary Wadding, organizing two CMA/medical mission teams to Zambia. On the last CMA/medical trip to Zambia we presented ten bicycles to pastors. You might wonder why we gave bicycles instead of motorcycles. Well, the closest gas station was two-and-a-half hours away so motorcycles would not be practical.

Going on these mission trips and seeing the living conditions of the people, the roads on which they must travel, and the distances between the many churches they oversee has been an inspiration to me. Each year I draw from my experiences on my mission trips to write letters, speaking from my heart, asking my family and friends to support RFS. Their response continues to be a blessing to me and to RFS.

I encourage everyone to participate in a mission trip. It will bring changes to your life in ways that you have never imagined–not short-term changes, but life-long changes. Your eyes will see differently, your ears will hear differently, your nose will smell differently, but most importantly, your heart will feel differently.

Below is a letter that was written by one of the pastors we worked with while on a mission trip.

17 July 2006
Dear Mission Team Member,
With thanks I greet you in the beloved name of our Lord Jesus Christ. Many people are very thankful for the job which you and your team did. Even the Headmen (leaders) of this place are pleased for that clinic, and they are all requesting you and your team to come again. Because of that clinic, it made many people to know Jesus Christ as their personal Saviour [sic]. And it made easier for me to follow-up the converts.

It was a good time for me to evangelise [sic] them. Me as a church leader I am requesting you to bring Jesus Film for more evangelism. We as a church we are praying for you every day for God to bless you and your ministry. So that God can make it possible to come again. Headmen are also requesting to add some more people on that 100 people who had given medicine.

Tender and warm greetings to you. May God bless you all the time.
Yours faithful, Elder Honest Simbala

This letter shows you just how much they appreciated the mission team and how great the need is for people to come and serve. As you can see, their main focus is evangelism. Because of the medical team, this pastor and others were able to meet many people and will now do follow-up visits to these villages. The team planted the seeds and now the pastors will water!

Then I heard the Lord asking, *"Whom should I send as a messenger to my people? Who will go for us?"* And I said, *"Lord, I'll go! Send me"* (Isaiah 6:8, NLT).

Are you willing to go?

Open Doors Trip - 2002[2]

Bob McClain, Texas, CMA No. 57,732

What a wonderful surprise it was to receive a phone call from Pat Meadows of Open Doors, USA one afternoon in July 2002. He informed me my name was one of six that had been drawn for a mission trip to visit the persecuted church in Chiapas, Mexico. I told him I would have to check with my employer to make sure there were no conflicts with my work schedule, and over the next few days, everything fell into place. I wondered why God would have chosen me for such a trip.

My amazement continued as I met the other team members in Dallas the evening before our flight. We had dinner together and shared how God was leading us to Mexico. We did not know that the people and experiences we were about to encounter would change our hearts forever.

As we got off the plane, we were met by Edgar. We boarded aged mini-vans and made our way to where we would stay—a hotel that was a restored Catholic convent. The owner was a very gracious host and invited us into his home for dinner one evening during the week.

That first evening at the hotel we met two local pastors who shared with us about their work in helping the persecuted Christians of that area. Both of the pastors are attorneys and are trying to secure the release of some thirty men imprisoned for murders they did not commit. We were also joined that evening by a young missionary named Mark Davis who worked with us throughout the week as a translator. We bonded with Mark and Edgar very quickly as we worked and worshipped with them.

The second evening we met Amy Lane whose daughter, Margaret, was the wife of the hotel owner. She came to

---

[2] All names have been changed.

Mexico in 1948 as a missionary from another country. An amazing woman, Amy shared with us from her vast experience and knowledge of the area and its people. On the last day of our visit, she showed us the missionary training center near Ocosingo. For a number of years the center had been closed due to political unrest and persecution of the Christians. The center was under restoration and we were able to eat and fellowship with some of the Indians working there. Amy called on the camp pastor to lead us in prayer for the noon meal. He began to pray, but choked up and grew silent. After a time, he regained his composure and completed the prayer. Amy explained to us that he was saved there when he was six years old and he had been praying for years that one day there would be missionaries seated at his table. Oh, does it touch your heart!

During the week we visited churches in several communities. We helped prepare for the construction of a greenhouse near Betania. The local pastor took us up the hillside to show us their main water source. There was a large hole in the ground with spring water gushing out of it. He told us there had been no water coming from it for a period of four years and they were suffering greatly because of it. One day the church members gathered around the hole and had a worship service. Soon it began to rain and water started flowing from the ground again and has not stopped since! They consequently renamed their village.

We traveled to the Chenalho area of Acteal to visit with Pastor Jose and the women of the local church. The church was protected by barbed concertina wire and two federal soldiers with rifles. Twenty-four of the women had husbands locked up in prison on false charges brought against them by neighboring Indians. The imprisoned men had been wrongly blamed for some murders that had occurred nearby. Because the Christians will not participate in drug and alcohol trafficking and the prostitution of their wives and daughters, the secular communities drive them out of their homes and persecute them in numerous ways. In violation of the Mexican Constitution, the children of Christian families are not allowed to attend public schools in these areas. They are being home-schooled by their parents and the churches. We gave out sack lunches, candy, and balloons to these children.

We also visited a so-called church in another town where the tribal leaders were dominant. The church is not a place where Christians meet, but a place where lost and superstitious people enter to chant and wail as they sacrifice chickens to their gods and pour a drug called *posh* down the mouths of their sick loved ones. Hundreds of candles were burning on the floor, along the walls, and elsewhere. Green hay was loosely scattered on the concrete floor and there were puddles of a liquid poured out in front of the people as they knelt in worship. As we first entered the church I felt pressure hit my chest. It was as if we were in the presence of a hundred séances taking place at once. We did not cease to pray as we moved about the room and we did not tarry long. I have never felt the presence of so much evil. It was almost overwhelming. We are praying God will bring salvation to that community and that one day that building will be full of His Spirit! Please pray for these people!

One morning we were blessed to visit another church. The pastors shared with us how their church came into being. After getting saved in a town some eight miles away, he walked to this village day after day to witness to the people about Jesus. He and his Christian brothers were arrested on many occasions by the authorities for preaching the gospel. Finally they were allowed by the government to build a church and two homes at their present location. But the villagers hated them and came with guns, sticks, and machetes one evening to drive them out. A fight ensued and the Christians were greatly outnumbered. Suddenly the villagers turned and ran back to their homes with forty-five injured, some with gunshot wounds. But the Christians had no guns and only fifteen of them sustained injuries! In the confusion the villagers had begun fighting themselves! God protected His church!

In the months that followed, one of the tribal leaders of that village had a daughter who became gravely ill and in spite of multiple trips to the witch doctor her condition only grew worse. Someone suggested that if he would take her to the "Evangelicals" for prayer that she would be healed. In desperation they carried the sick child to the Christians and God healed her! The tribal leader broke down and gave his heart to the Lord and his property for a church to be built upon! Two years had passed at the time of our visit and the church was half built and some two hundred people had already come to Christ!

On our way back to the hotel, we stopped by to see Sister Penelope in Teopisca. She told us about God sparing her life one night after she received a shotgun blast to her face and torso, then crawling from her burning home. The enemy had come that night to destroy the entire family because of their faith in Christ. Penelope escaped alone but received a vision of the others in heaven while she recovered in the hospital. We purchased some of her hand-crafted items in support of her ministry.

The Christians in Chiapas, Mexico, will bless your heart! They shared their homes, their food, and their hearts with us. All they asked in return was that we pray for them and ask others to pray for them as well. The persecution of Christians here is the most severe in Mexico, and we found the New Testament Church to be alive and well! God is at work! Please pray for our brothers and sisters!

A Humbling Experience

Dave Miller, Virginia, CMA No. 18,151

I have been a member of CMA for the last 21 years. When it was announced that CMA was going to raise funds for overseas ministry, I was uncomfortable with that decision. I felt our calling was to minister to bikers on the streets of this country. The first year, I participated, but only enough to get a t-shirt. After the second year, it became apparent to me that God was moving through RFS, so I began to ask family and friends to support me. I raised about $500 that year, and received some incentives. I continued doing a little better each year.

In 1997, I was at a Seasons of Refreshing in Virginia when we were encouraged to go on a mission trip. I felt an urging in my spirit, so I told God, "If you want me to go on a mission trip, you'll have to provide the funds, because I don't have the money to go." I made a verbal commitment there at Seasons and during the next coffee break, a member came up to me and handed me $100. He told me he felt led to give me "seed money" for the trip, and I was to tithe 10% and use the rest for the mission trip. This was my sign that I was to go on a mission trip. I saved up as much as I could and received some help from my church. It took about $1,000 by the time I got my passport and health shots.

When the time came for the trip, I drove to Florida and met our team leader, Gary Wadding. The next day, we went to the Miami airport where we met the other CMA members who were excited about the trip. There were nine in all. We left on the trip on my 50th birthday and Vicky, Gary's wife, prepared a birthday dinner of lasagna. Wow! What a treat!

The airplane we boarded at the Aviateca Airlines terminal was a Taca Airlines plane; we called it "Taco Airlines." We left a little after 4 p.m., and after stops in Guatemala and San Salvador, we arrived in Managua, Nicaragua. We walked over

101

to the customs desk and were greeted by soldiers carrying automatic weapons. It took us about three hours to clear customs; we were getting really tired by this time. We were taken to the home of Accrual Ibarra and his lovely wife, Martha, our hosts. Their house and yard, surrounded by a tall block fence, had been turned into a mission compound. There were beautiful bird-of-paradise plants and lime trees in the front yard. Attached to the house were bunkrooms and an almost-modern bathhouse.

The next day we all boarded a big yellow school bus. I thought it was neat that the bus was made in Virginia, just thirty miles from my home. We were headed out to Chinandega to present a bike to Pastor Carlos Ramero. He was a really nice twenty-seven-year-old pastor with a tiny white church that had an attached room where he and his family lived. Their room was about 12'x12' and housed him, his wife, and two children. Carlos cried when we presented the motorcycle to him.

Our next day was for relaxation—of sorts. We toured an active volcano called "The Gateway to Hell." It was a massive mountain with a lava field of about four miles. We also toured a museum at the foot of the volcano. They told us about how the Indians sacrificed maidens and small children in the volcano. We went to the market (about a forty-minute ride), which looked similar to one of our flea markets. We were warned to take off any jewelry and watches, and to put our wallets in front pockets (to avoid being robbed). Thus protected, we ventured into the market place and bought some souvenirs. There were young children everywhere who wanted to be our guides at the marketplace. They all wanted a little money to buy shoes so they could go to school, as there was a law that required the children to wear shoes in order to attend school. I'm sure we helped a dozen or so kids make it to school.

The next trip was a nighttime visit to Pastor Carlos Castillo's church. We were all up on the stage preparing to sing "This Little Light of Mine" when the power went off in that whole sector of the city! Each of the guys had mini Maglite® flashlights and we screwed the heads off and it looked like we were holding candles! God must have a sense of humor! The church service went on as if nothing had happened. We presented the motorcycle to the pastor and prayed over him.

Our next trip was out away from the city in a little village. There was an eerie feeling of some kind of evil all through this village. It was one of those things that made the hair on the back of my neck stand up! Hardly any of the men who lived in the village came to the church service. It was really neat to watch one of our team members ride the bike into the church at the beginning of the service. We laid hands on the pastor and prayed for him and his motorcycle.

After returning home from this mission trip, I had a sense of being humbled. We have so much here in America and those believers down in Nicaragua have so little. This trip gave me a whole new outlook on RFS and gave me a desire to raise as much money as I can for the run. I have been there and done that! You too can experience the joy of helping other believers by providing motorcycles, Bibles, and the *JESUS* film. If you have never gone on a mission trip, I personally challenge you to make that commitment to the Lord, and experience the blessings I've shared with you!

Appreciate the Small Things

Dennis Forry, Pennsylvania, CMA No. 49,890

To raise money for RFS, I sent out letters to family, friends, and business associates explaining what CMA means to me and how RFS is an important part of my commitment to CMA. I told people my financial goal for the year and that I had a contributor who promised to match all donations up to $2,500. I also included an RFS brochure and a self-addressed, stamped envelope. Then I sent 'thank you' notes to everyone who contributed.

In November 2005, I was privileged to go on a mission trip to Guatemala. After I returned from Guatemala, I sent the following letter to the people who had contributed to RFS.

Dear Family and Friends,

I had a great time in Guatemala. It was an experience I will never forget. I will try to put into words some of the things I did and things I experienced.

On Friday, November 4, I flew from Baltimore to Houston and met some of our team at the hotel, where we had lunch. I found a dead bee in my soup, and thought that maybe this was preparing me for my trip! My luggage was three pounds overweight so I went to the store to buy a bag to carry on the plane. I told the sales clerk that I wanted a bag similar to the one she was using. But they didn't have anything like it in the store, so she emptied her bag and gave it to me. I tried to pay her for it, but she wouldn't accept anything because it was for a good cause in Guatemala.

On Saturday morning we met the rest of our team at the Houston airport. There were thirteen of us on the team (9 men and 4 women). We flew to Guatemala City where we were met by Randy and Brenda Purcell. They and their three children are missionaries living in the city. They took us to their home and gave us a sack lunch. We loaded a pickup truck with a motorcycle and our luggage and drove four hours to Santa Cruz Del Quiche to spend the night. We traveled in an eleven-passenger van. With Randy Purcell and Rene Gonzalez there were fifteen of us so four people rode in the truck. We were all very cramped. We had our orientation meeting in the courtyard at the hotel.

Sunday morning we had devotions and left the hotel to drive three more hours to the city of Nebaj. Nebaj has a population of 110,000 and sits at an elevation of 9,842 feet. The dirt road to Nebaj was steep and narrow, and had no guardrails. At one point we were at an elevation of over 13,000 feet. The towns we passed through had cobblestone streets with lots of speed bumps. I got to ride the 200cc Yamaha motorcycle for the last half of the trip, and I was covered with mud when we got to our destination.

Sunday afternoon we presented our first bike to Pastor Manolo De Valle. In Guatemala the Sunday services are in the afternoon. We were given a time at the beginning of the service to present the bike, helmet, stickers, t-shirts, and bag to the pastor and his wife. We used several team members to make the presentation and to pray for the pastor and dedicate his bike. The church was very nice and there were about 400 people present. Praise and worship was a large part of the service and the congregation was joyful and animated in their singing. The pastor preached with an interpreter because the city has two languages, Spanish and Mayan. At the end of the service, which lasted three-and-a-half hours, we participated in communion. It was all a wonderful and very worshipful experience for me.

The women bunked at the hospital and the men stayed at a men's drug and alcohol rehab center. Each room had 2 sets of bunk beds and two chairs. We had no heat. It went down to 39° one night. The restrooms had only cold water at the sink and "widow makers" on the showerhead for lukewarm water. A widow maker is an electric heating element used to heat the water as you take a shower, but it doesn't work very well. We could not to flush the toilet paper because the sewer system couldn't handle it, nor could we drink the water because it would make us sick.

Monday and Tuesday were spent at the hospital cleaning and painting the outside walls. Some of us worked on the electrical wiring for the fluorescent lights inside the hospital and on the porches. We also got their generator running again. We had to work between showers of light rain for the whole two days. We went into each room of the hospital and prayed over it.

Wednesday morning, three of our team woke up feeling sick, and remained sick all day. After our morning devotions and breakfast, we loaded our bags and left Nebaj for a long eight-hour drive back to [the] Missionary Ventures International (MVI) Mission House in San Lucas. God is good! He kept His protecting hand over us on those rough, narrow, dirt roads. Guatemalan drivers are crazy! They pass on blind curves and anywhere else they feel like it. We were sitting in a restaurant for supper when a car crashed right outside and sheared off a telephone pole. We thought the car was coming through the building. It was wonderful to be at the mission house. We had hot water, nice showers, carpeted floors, and even got to flush the toilet paper!

Thursday morning, we got an early start. After devotions and breakfast, we traveled to Santa Lucia to present our second motorcycle. This bike was given to Pastor Alejandro Molina Xicay, a spry 61-year-old man. I had the privilege to pray for this pastor and bike. Four more people in our group were sick this day. From Santa Lucia we drove to the beach in San Jose Puerto. Along the way, we stopped at a restaurant and had hamburgers, but it was the strangest tasting hamburger I've ever had. I'm not sure I want to know what it was really made of! When we got to the beach, an armed guard escorted us because they had been having trouble with armed robberies in the area. The sand at this beach was black due to local volcanoes. Some of our team members introduced the guard and two of his friends to the Lord, and they placed their faith in

Christ as they knelt on the black sand and prayed. Praise the Lord! What an experience! We left the beach and traveled to a church and feeding center where we met Pastor Miguel and his family. Pastor Miguel leads the church and runs the feeding center where they feed about 150 children three days a week. We hurried back to Guatemala City to pick up the third motorcycle and present it to Pastor Carlos Oswaldo Valladares Asencio. We presented this motorcycle during a break in the Thursday evening Bible study. After the service, they fed the whole church chicken tamales and a pineapple drink.

Friday morning, we men went to a drug and alcohol rehab center for men in a bad section of Guatemala City. The businesses in this section of town must pay the gangs for protection. We met Pastor Ed, director of the facility, who also has a store in the front of the building to help supplement funds for the center. We met and prayed over many of the men. One man at the center is so grateful to them that he gets up every morning at 4:30 to go to the outdoor market. He goes from vendor to vendor to get free produce. Every day he brings back two large bags of food to feed all the men in the rehab center. Another man at the center doesn't want to leave, so he spends the day on the roof preparing the food and cooking for the men. While we were there, a family of eight came to visit one of the men, and some of our team led all eight of them to Christ. What an experience!

After the rehab center, we went to a Harley Davidson shop to buy some goodies. Next, we traveled to Antigua to meet the women from our group who had spent the day shopping. We bought gifts to take home to our families. Antigua is a tourist town, so there were hundreds of stands selling mostly handcrafted items made in Guatemala.

Randy and Brenda Purcell took us to a huge old convent that was built in the 1500s. The convent has been made into a five-star hotel/restaurant. We were served a very nice dinner at the restaurant to thank us for all the work we did. When we finished eating we had the privilege of taking a little tour of the place. It was beautiful, and because it was dark, they had the place lit up with candles.

Friday night we all got together to talk about what this trip meant to us. We sang some songs and ate the Lord's Supper together.

Saturday morning, after packing our suitcases, we enjoyed a tasty breakfast and had our morning devotions. We presented Randy and Brenda Purcell, our hosts, with a monetary gift from our team. We loaded our bags into the pickup truck and went to the Guatemala City airport. We had an uneventful flight back to Houston.

This trip was an unforgettable experience for me! The people were very friendly; waving at us as we drove by. They have very few material possessions, yet they shared with us everything they had. The children didn't have much to play with, but they were happy. I wanted to bring them home with me. The church services were alive and the people participated whole-heartedly. They didn't watch the time or worry about when the service would be over. The country of Guatemala is a very beautiful place and the people are special and hungry for the Word of God.

Our mission team came from all over the United States from different walks of life, but we all share[d] a common bond. We all love our Savior, and have a passion to reach the unsaved for Christ. We also enjoy motorcycling. Our team enjoyed a special closeness and worked very well together. We spent a lot of time traveling in cramped quarters in the van, but it gave us a great opportunity to get to know each other. Our group devotions in the mornings were a very special time, and we had several occasions to pray for many people, as well as for each other. This trip was a life-changing experience for me, and I hope it will be reflected in my words and actions to the people around me. If I get another opportunity, I will go again!

I recommend a trip like this for everyone. It opened my eyes to the way another part of the world lives, and hopefully, it will cause me to be more appreciative of the things with which I have been blessed.

Miracles in Peru

Don Potter, Texas, CMA No. 43,516

I was sitting at a Seasons of Refreshing, blessed of God, while Curtis Clements preached, telling of a mission trip to Peru. He said, "This trip is not for the unhealthy or faint of heart. I need men only, with construction experience, who can handle the heat. We will be going upriver in the Amazon River Basin to a small village to help build a church." I've been in roofing and remodeling for over twenty years, and God spoke to my heart to volunteer. Though financially strapped, my wife, Susan, reminded me that God would provide.

After 9/11/01, my business had been very slow and I did not have the money for this trip. After much prayer wondering how I could do this, my former pastor asked me to preach a Sunday morning service and present the need. The full amount was raised, including what I needed for vaccinations and spending money. I had enough for the trip! The kids in our church gathered candy, toy jewelry, and pocket crosses for me to take. I was prepared!

On November 7, 2003, when I was on a plane from Houston bound for Lima, Peru, fear came over me–fear of flying combined with a brochure that warned us not to leave major cities or go to remote villages because of drug activity and military unrest. I prayed, "Lord, my life is in your hands; even if this plane crashes it won't matter because you are in control of my destiny." Peace came over me that lasted for the duration of the trip; I was acutely aware of God's presence.

We arrived in Lima, Peru, at 11:30 p.m. By the time we settled in our hotel room it was very late. The noise in the street and sirens kept us awake even longer. I won't even tell about the activity in the street below our hotel room window– and this was the better side of town.

Early the next morning after breakfast at a sidewalk café we were on a plane to Tarapoto. We went from Lima (population, 9 million) over the Andes Mountains to Tarapoto, about 50,000 people.

This particular night we went to a church service where we were to present a 200cc dirt bike to the pastor. I felt the overwhelming presence of the Holy Spirit as we entered. They were singing praise (in Spanish, of course). Though I didn't understand the words, I felt so blessed in this worship I could not contain my emotions. The tears flowed freely. I stood there weeping and praising God when Curtis handed me the keys to the bike. "Would you present the bike to the pastor?" he asked. I'm not sure whether he asked me because he saw I was so touched by God or to get me under control by giving me something to do.

Having never done anything like this it did get my focus off worship to fervent prayer. "Lord, help me know what to say, dry my tears, and empower me to do this." With Angel Oyola from Missionary Ventures translating, God led me to say, "The key to this bike represents the key to the hearts of your people that you will reach with the gospel of Jesus Christ." It was at that moment I felt I was standing in the perfect will of God.

The next day we landed in Yurimagaus, population, 10,000. The airport was crowded with people to see the jet plane. They had just extended the runway to accommodate a small jet airliner which landed twice a week.

We then gathered supplies and boarded a boat on the Huallaga River. It was a narrow boat about 60 feet long with a 60hp motor. The live chickens we brought (which I thought were a gift for the villagers) turned out to be lunch and dinner for us for the next three days.

We traveled upriver for about five hours to the remote village of Frey Martin. I had never been so far away from civilization in my life. We passed rafts and small boats loaded with bananas, livestock, and other items, floating down the river to market in Yurimagaus.

We rounded a bend and there it was, the village of Frey Martin, beautiful green rolling hills, a tropical paradise. We were greeted at the shoreline by the pastor's children—about

110

eight of the most beautiful children I'd ever seen. I had a feeling of déjà vu, like maybe I had dreamed this before. My euphoria was slightly quenched as we carried our gear about ¼ of a mile up a trail from the riverbank to the hut where we set up camp. The hut had two bamboo walls and a thatched roof with four tents underneath where the ten of us slept.

It was hot. We got water for baths by dropping a bucket into a well. I began to sweat again as we sat down to a supper of fresh-killed chicken and fried banana. A young lady from Yurimagaus was hired to cook for us and did an excellent job. (I don't know how many of us could kill and cook a chicken.)

The next morning we carried tools, drinking water, etc. about ¾ of a mile to the other side of the village to work on building a church. When we got there we realized we had to mix concrete for the slab. The hard part was that there was no concrete mixer. We had to use short-handled shovels to mix the concrete and carry the water from a pond about ¼ of a mile downhill. Unfortunately, we emptied the small spring-fed pond that day, which meant the nearest water supply was then twice as far. That night it rained, filling the pond, which gave us enough water for the next two days!

This was the second miracle. The first miracle was my being there to begin with. The third miracle came the last day when we gathered all the candy we had brought and bagged it to give to the children. We had 69 bags of candy when we went to the school to visit with the kids. Angel and Mary with MVI witnessed to them and we handed out the candy. It looked like we had just enough, then they brought the rest of the kids in. You could see the look of panic in our eyes as the bags were handed out. At the end of the candy one little girl cried because she had none. An older child confessed he had taken two, and he handed her one. Every child had one! I estimated between 80-90 children. You do the math. Praise God! Thank you, Curtis, and all CMAers, for your faithfulness to continue these mission trips. Thank you, Lord.

The Rock

Glenn Strutton, Texas, CMA No. 56,986

In 2005, my wife Janice and I went to Bolivia with Curtis Clements and a group of CMA members. While we were there we worked hard, but everywhere we looked, there were local people working right along with us.

At one point, we did some evangelism. We divided the town into sections, split up our team with different translators, and went out to knock on doors. We told the people why we were there and invited them to the church where Curtis would be preaching.

We were talking to a young mother about coming to the church service when her husband walked into the yard. He wasn't very happy to see a group of "gringos" standing in his yard talking to his wife. But after our translator explained why we were there, he settled down. We asked him to come to the church service, but he said he couldn't go to church. Through our translator, I asked him why he couldn't go to church and he said he had a problem with alcohol. (Alcoholism is a huge problem in Bolivia.) This really hit home with me because I once had a "problem" with alcohol myself. Jose Murillo, our translator, asked him if I could pray for him. He said yes, and we proceeded to pray. This was the first time I had ever heard one of my prayers translated into a different language. After our prayer, I took one of the little red stones and put it in his hand. I told him that for many years, I had had a problem with alcohol and the way I kicked it was through Jesus. I asked him to keep the rock in his pocket all the time and every time he felt like he needed a drink, to just pull out the stone, think about Jesus, and say a prayer. There was nothing magic about the rock or anything like that, and that he might even still take the drink. But eventually Jesus would work through his prayers to help him get stronger.

The next night that young man came forward and accepted the Lord as his Savior, along with about forty teenagers, and several others.

We serve an Awesome God! I was able to take something as simple as a little red rock and work through it to bring someone closer to Jesus. By the way, through all of the praying and translating, Jose Murillo, our translator, realized he was not saved either. Before we left, Jose and his wife, Carola, prayed and turned their lives over to the Lord also. Thank You, Jesus!

Improving the Quality of Life

Joe & Corene Crouse, Texas, CMA Nos. 80,859 & 80,860

Does God have a use for you? We asked that question when we joined CMA in 2001. We have seen the answer.

Each year since 2001, we have raised money and participated in RFS. But we didn't understand the enormous difference a few dollars can make in the life of a struggling pastor until we went on a CMA mission trip. We have been on two mission trips in the last three years, and both were to Zambia, Africa, as part of a medical mission trip.

We saw firsthand how a simple bicycle can improve the life of a pastor. Transportation makes it possible for the pastor not only to spend more time with his family, but also enables him to see his flock easier, and attend classes. Many of the pastors cry tears of joy and say they have been praying many years for a bicycle. They praise God for this wonderful blessing brought by Christian brothers and sisters.

It is difficult to describe the joy of people who see the *JESUS* film in their own language or for us to comprehend that hundreds of people would walk miles and sit on the cold ground (many with no coats) just to see the film. It blessed us to hear the crowd react with awe at the fish being brought into the boat, to see their tears as they come forward after the film to ask Jesus to be their Savior. How much is one soul worth? How much for 100 souls?

We visited churches on the first trip and were blessed by the Christian fellowship. Our interpreters did their best to clarify communication since most of the Tonga people do not speak English and none of us spoke Tonga. We did not need to have an interpreter, however, to understand and feel the Holy Spirit's presence.

The medical care we provided was very basic at best—mostly vitamins, wormers, and some antibiotics. We could not treat most of the problems we saw, as we did not have the

114

equipment or medication. It was very humbling to know that only God could help these people. The prayer station was the most important station we set up, as only there did these people receive what they had come for—spiritual healing.

On the last trip, we saw over 715 people in the medical clinic, and we prayed for every single person. Over 300 committed (and 100 rededicated) their lives to Jesus. Some had never heard the Good News of Jesus Christ. At the prayer station many of the older people said they did not know they could have a relationship with Jesus Christ.

We challenge each of you to try to make at least one mission trip in your life. We didn't think there was any way that we could financially go (a clever deception of the dark one). We prayed and we mentioned the trip to our local church, which was very supportive.

Many of the people in several of the local churches and CMA took up the call to be prayer warriors throughout our several months of planning and during the trip. *This firm foundation made everything possible.* We collected vitamins and medications brought in each week by church members. The local ministerial alliance had a community-wide dinner to raise funds for our trip. Our local CMA chapter had a dinner and yard sale to help with our costs. We visited each church that supported us, both before and after the trip. This does not mean there were not roadblocks and a few brick walls in our way. However, each barrier miraculously came down just in time for everything we needed.

Packing Light

Linda Buchanan, Texas, CMA No. 74,135

My husband, Rick, and I joined CMA in January 2000. In June, we went to the Honda Hoot in North Carolina. You should have seen us on that trip! I had everything but the washing machine and the kitchen sink bungee-corded to the back of that poor Honda Shadow! My husband almost earned the road name of "Bungee Cord King"! It is a wonder we got there and back with all that "stuff." On our way back to Texas, we thought we would check out the CMA National Rally. We stopped for gas east of Mena, Arkansas and met Steve Beam with MVI.

At the rally, we met many wonderful people and were really pumped up about being part of CMA. When I learned we could participate in a mission trip and help deliver motorcycles, I said, "Sign me up!" even though I didn't know how we could afford it. Well, God provided the resources before the due date and I was off with Curtis Clements and a group to Oax-aca, Mexico! They gave us a list of suggested things to pack into ONE bag; then we could take a piece of carry-on luggage. I had one BIG bag, with wheels on the bottom, my carry-on, and my purse. We checked the luggage in Dallas, flew to Houston, met the rest of the group, and then flew to Mexico City. It was in Mexico City that we realized that everyone's bag made it but mine. We checked, we waited, and then we had to talk to the authorities at the airport and board our bus. I still had my carry-on and my purse: let's see—medicine, check! makeup, check! money, check! toiletries, check! I was wearing jeans, boots, and a t-shirt. We checked on my luggage again the morning after our arrival—still no BIG bag. There was no mall in Oaxaca City, we had a tight schedule, and I did not want to hold anyone up, so we decided to go on without my bag.

Everyone was gracious. I borrowed a t-shirt from probably every man in the group. The ladies were helpful in lending me skirts, since in Mexico pants are unacceptable for ladies. My boots worked fine for the trip and I washed out socks and undies every night. My roommate, Rosie, even shared some unmentionables with me. I made it just fine!

We had a great time and we met the most wonderful people! We saw so many people who shared with us what little food they had. They lived in thatch huts with dirt floors, sharing the space with chickens. They wore the only clothes they had and they were content and happy to belong to the Lord. We shed tears as pastors accepted their keys to a motorcycle and helmet with a CMA sticker on it. We heard scripture recited in Spanish in a little adobe church with wooden benches and a dirt floor. We heard hymns sung in Spanish that were so beautiful they brought tears again. The people of Oaxaca City were pleased we came to spend time with them. And we were thankful to have the opportunity.

At the end of the week, we walked through the marketplace in Oaxaca City where Rosie and I bought Mexican dresses as mementoes of the trip. We checked once more at the airport for my bag–it was there! The next morning Curtis and I lugged it all the way back to Dallas.

From then on, I have been able to travel with Rick on the motorcycle without ANY bungee cords. We can pack all we need in the saddlebags, trunk, and T-bag. AND, I have only been to the mall to buy Christmas presents for my family and my friends! If you ever have an opportunity to go on a mission trip with one of the evangelists, I encourage you to do so. May you be blessed and be a blessing!

The Great Commission

Loretta Owens, Louisiana, CMA No. 90,464

Welcome to Nineveh! I felt like Jonah must have felt basking in the sun on a beach in a strange and foreign land, with seaweed hanging from his head. Motorcycles are the last thing on earth I would have ever thought I would have anything to do with!

God has a wonderful sense of humor and takes us places we never could imagine. It all started when we found a welcome place of refuge under a tent where people were serving cold water at the 2002 Republic of Texas Rally in Austin, Texas. We saved the cup as I thought we could use that idea at home. Then, in a leather shop, we were given a *Hope for the Highway* New Testament. The message on the back cover was exciting and powerful–an open invitation for the ride of your life! I was touched. At the Charlie Daniels concert Saturday night, Charlie thanked CMA for handling registration. There were over 40,000 people registered and no one had stood in line over three minutes! I looked at Jim and said, "I can pass out water and I can work registration."

Monday morning Jim called CMA headquarters in Hatfield, Arkansas, to learn more about CMA. He was told there was a chapter in our hometown! I didn't want to go to any meetings or have any responsibilities; I just wanted to go when it was "convenient." I could just go in my suburban and help occasionally.

That summer on our way to the Sturgis South Rally in Sturgis, Mississippi, Jim and I listened to the Ministry Team Training tapes and I took the time to read a *HeartBeat*. I was really impressed with the training they provided and with the God-centeredness I observed. By then I had gone to a meeting with Jim and I found a real mix of people that I loved– they had taken me in. Somewhere along the way I read about RFS. I learned that every dollar given goes to missions and

118

that for every dollar given a soul is saved. I learned that native pastors were being given motorcycles. All this got my attention! I was gripped by those facts. This was a rare opportunity to invest in eternal treasure! Every dollar given used for missions! Wow! I knew God could use me. I could help Jim write to family and friends to get "sponsors" for a 100-mile ride. RFS became my passion!

When we went to a rally on Iron Mountain we heard "Stories of Jesus" that our ministry partners told. Giving motorcycles to native pastors was just one part! I was in awe of how God had called Jim and me to be a part of this ministry and how He could engage our family and friends in *changing the world, one heart at a time.*

Jim has been on two mission trips: to Honduras in 2004, and to Bolivia in 2005. I went with him in spirit because I prayed for their group and thought about them constantly. When he got home, I listened for hours to the "stories of Jesus" that I love to hear - stories of people...stories of God at work...stories that captured my heart.

Run for the Son is an awesome opportunity to help fulfill "The Great Commission."

From Trash to Treasure

Dan Schumacher, Minnesota, CMA No. 61,998

I joined CMA in 1997 after receiving Christ on the Spring Flood Run in Minnesota, thanks to the Lord and faithful CMAers who were there when I needed them. God is so good! At the Seasons of Refreshing in 1999, I learned of the upcoming mission trip to Nicaragua with Dan Fitzpatrick [former CMA Evangelist]. As you all know, when God calls, you'd better listen, and I knew right away I was to go on that mission trip. Once God calls He, never rescinds that call and we either do what He says or He may not ask us to do anything else, much to our spiritual loss. So I made the necessary calls, got the information, and was put on the list to go.

Preparations for the trip required a series of shots for various diseases. My apprehension began to surface as I learned of the nasty bugs that the region offers unsuspecting travelers. The packet of info I received from CMA and MVI stressed the need for prayer for the mission's success, so I began to pray for protection and for all aspects of the trip to be fruitful. I knew the Lord would be in control and to God's praise, we had perfect weather the whole trip. There were no problems except for one lost piece of luggage when we got back to Houston.

Our flight left Houston with twelve members from seven states: Minnesota, Iowa, Nebraska, Missouri, Colorado, Washington, and Maryland. We got to know each other along the way, starting at the airport and continuing throughout the trip. We flew from Houston to San Salvador, with a stop in Belize, and on to Managua, Nicaragua, where we were met by our host Eric Loftsgard and another missionary, Sondra Livermore. Eric drove a 15-passenger van, thus the need to keep teams to twelve people, with room for an interpreter or two. Eric had a wife and five kids that ranged in age from one-and-a-half to eleven years. They lived about ten miles outside of Managua and had been called by God to go back to Nicaragua after going there for a mission trip some time before. Eric not only hosted visiting mission teams, but was actively involved in building projects for churches he served, among other ministries.

The house we stayed in belonged to a doctor and had been added on to by other CMA mission teams. They had added four showers and toilets and three bunkhouse rooms, creating a living area just for mission teams. There was no running hot water, as electricity was expensive, so conservation was essential. They had two cooks who provided us with all our meals. I felt guilty having so much to eat when most of the people we met on the trip had so little. The house was part of a compound surrounded by a concrete wall topped with razor wire. Thefts had taken place before so they needed some protection. All vehicles were parked inside the compound as well.

Sondra, the other missionary who helped us while there, told us about the corrupt police and political system in Nicaragua. Wages and salaries were so low there that all those in power relied on a system of bribery in order to extract money for themselves. Sondra had been ticketed numerous times in her car, for alleged traffic violations. The first time she got a ticket she refused to pay a bribe and as a result was detained, had her license taken away, was solicited for sex, and eventually had to get someone from the embassy to get her license back. It took months to do that and only was achieved after an official was bribed. She was told to pay the bribe the next time because there was no getting around the corrupt system. The country was so impoverished that police would respond to a call only if they received gas money from whoever called. That was why we would see armed guards at many of the businesses, because they could not rely on the police to respond to calls.

Managua was an interesting city. There were no street signs anywhere. Reference points were used to find places, some of which were no longer there. For instance, "...go to where the old blacksmith shop used to be and turn right." There was virtually no road maintenance so we had to swerve around potholes and avoid ruts constantly. One pothole we saw was so huge you could have lost a small car in it. It was interesting to see the many shacks, made of tin and plywood with thatched roofs, with an electric meter on the side and power running into them. Right across the street from our compound were those kinds of shacks, with dirt yards that the owners would sweep to remove debris. Amidst all this poverty was the new palatial mansion being built for the president, complete with a multi-colored fountain in the square in front of the palace.

The people of Nicaragua have had a tough time for a long while. When communism was the rule they were used to everything being given them for nothing, but there were a lot of labor skills handed down from generation to generation. During the Contra war many of these skills were put on hold, as fighting became the rule, rather than the exception. As a result, labor skills skipped a generation or so and the knowledge needed to build things was lost. To add to this, natural disasters became numerous and relief agencies began pouring in, giving the people everything they could. As a result of these things, the people lost much of the ability to provide for themselves.

In spite of all these natural disasters, the dedicated missionaries and pastors continue to bring the message of hope through the gospel of our Lord and Savior, Jesus Christ. Relief agencies provide physical needs and Jesus provides hope. Through MVI, CMA gave away four motorcycles to pastors in the area. One traveled all the way from the Mosquito Coast (350km) to receive his bike and had to ride for about 24 hours to get back home. On part of his trip back home, he had to put the bike on boats or canoes to cross the flooded rivers and streams because a recent hurricane had hit the area and taken out most of the bridges. This pastor, Alliston Perez, was overseeing eleven congregations and was soon to be adding two more. The motorcycle he received allowed him to visit the churches he was overseeing within a much shorter time. He had been walking most of the time, but would now be able to ride. It says in 1 Peter that we have the ability, or power, to hasten the return of Christ. No one knows when He will return, but each person we tell of the gospel message brings us that much closer to His return. When God determines that all have heard the gospel, or the last saint has been rejoiced over by angels or the last martyr has died for Christ, or whatever God's timetable may be, Christ will return. Many things must take place before then, but each day brings us closer to His coming. These motorcycles that CMA gives away help to hasten that glorious day by allowing His servants to reach the lost quicker.

The most unforgettable moment of the mission trip to Nicaragua was our trip to the city dump. One of the pastors who received a bike also had a school on the church property for the children of the families who lived in the city dump. Every day the pastor and his group would prepare and deliver a noon meal to the dump for the children who lived there. We were honored to be able to go with them to help serve the meal to the children. Some of the children had open sores on their bodies and obvious signs of malnutrition. (Loss of pigmentation to the skin and light coloring of their hair would eventually go away as they continued to eat the meals the pastor and his church provided.) One of the children we served had to be hand-fed because he was so weak that he couldn't eat by himself. These kids, about eighty of them in all, waited patiently while one of the missionaries gave them their spiritual lesson for the day, and even waited while one of our group members spoke to them through an interpreter. With the huge mountain of garbage looming in the distance and the makeshift shacks right next to them, these children ate a nutritious meal the Lord provided for them. Two of our team members were struggling to keep the flies off the food until the children received it, and believe me, that was a chore. The shacks the families lived in were put together with nothing more than materials other people had thrown away. We were allowed to look into one of the shacks and there on the makeshift "kitchen" table was a tattered, open Bible. God bless them!

That evening our team went to a restaurant that specialized in ice cream desserts and I found it hard to enjoy what I ordered when thinking back on the day's events. What I learned through this trip, and especially through the time at the city dump, was that I have so very much to be thankful for when others around the world exist only on what other people throw away. God has blessed me with abundance and I am to take nothing for granted, giving Him praise and honor and glory at all times. I must be generous with what I have because it all belongs to God anyway.

We gave away four motorcycles and each of the pastors who received them has my utmost respect. I was humbled to stand in their presence. I was fortunate to be able to speak a few words to the group when we presented one of the bikes and was allowed to ride one of the other bikes to the church where we gave it away. Each one of these humble pastors that received the bikes touched my heart and soul with their dedication to the Lord.

The Healing Power of Prayer

Victoria Bowers, Florida, 74,431

It was dusk in the Philippines when the jeepney came to pick us up and take us to the church. We were a group of CMA members leading a Pastors Conference. I preached that afternoon on the Power of Prayer, and was feeling tired and eager to see the video so I could hear what the Holy Spirit had said through me. By the time the church service started, it was very late and I simply wished that I were back in my room asleep.

The service started with a couple of songs, and then had a time of greeting each other in the Lord while we sang a fellowship song. I gradually made my way to the rather empty entryway at the back of the church. A lovely young lady by the name of Violy greeted me. I had prayed for her at the altar on my first night here. She grabbed my hand in hers. "Pray for me," she whispered; "I have the fever." She placed the back of my hand against her neck. It felt like it was in a furnace heated up seven times hotter. I almost expected to see it burst into flames because her neck was so hot. Immediately I drew her close, threw my arms around her, and with my mouth close to her ear, I prayed the believer's prayer: *"Father, I stand in obedience to Your Word, laying my hands upon the sick. Thank You that You bless all the work of my hands. Thank You that Jesus already paid for Violy's healing by the wounds He bore at Calvary. Thank You for being faithful to perform what You have said in Your Word. I plead the blood of Jesus over Violy, and pray this prayer in the mighty name of Jesus, the anointed. Amen."*

Nothing happened. I gently kissed her check and returned to my seat as praise and worship resumed. My thoughts were racing. 'Why, Lord? Why didn't You heal her? Aren't You listening? Don't You know that I preached this afternoon on the power of Prayer? You're supposed to be listening to and answering my prayers. I'm so embarrassed. I'm not going to tell anyone I prayed for Violy. I hope she won't tell anyone either.' I was restless, struggling with these thoughts and wishing I had not come to the meeting because then I would not have been struggling with the lack of power in my prayers. Suddenly, I straightened up. 'God,' I breathed, 'I don't care. I don't care that I'm tired. I don't care if You answer my prayers or not. I believe that You are who You say You are. I'm going to praise You no matter what, because You are worthy of praise.'

And I did. I praised God with every ounce of energy I had. I clapped, I wept, I danced (somewhat). I moved out of my seat and up into the altar area where I had more room to move. So what if people were watching me. This was between God and me. I needed to be at the altar praising and worshiping Him. I gave it my all without knowing if He paid any attention or gave me any notice.

The next morning, Violy was the first person I saw when I arrived at church. And the first words out of her mouth were, "Our God is a God of miracles." Again, she took my hand and placed it against her neck. She felt as cool as a watermelon just taken out of the refrigerator. "Wow, God!" I breathed. "Thank You. Please forgive me for having doubted and gotten upset. I was wrong."

When I got home and recovered from jetlag, I read in 2 Chronicles 20 where people came and told King Jehoshaphat that a great multitude was coming against him. Jehoshaphat feared and set himself to seek the Lord. In verse 20, he lines up the army to go out to battle, but in front of the warriors, he placed the singers armed only with songs of praise to the Lord. And they went out to meet the enemy with a song on their lips. Verse 22 says, *Now when they began to sing and to praise, the Lord set ambushes against the people...who had come against Judah; and they were defeated (NKJV).*

When were they defeated? When did God answer Jehoshaphat's prayer? When the singers began to praise!

I finally got to watch myself preach on video. (Remember that I had preached the afternoon before I prayed for Violy.) And do you know what I said was the key to unlock the power of prayer? The key to unlock the power of prayer is praise, because God inhabits the praises of His people. And the sacrifice of praise–praising God when you don't feel like it–unleashes an extra dose of power.

I preached it, I experienced it, I read about it in the Word of God, and then I heard it on video. God must really want this to come alive in me. So, my advice to you is to praise God. Praise Him when you want to; praise Him when you don't feel like it. Praise Him in every circumstance. When you praise Him, He will be there, and He will answer.

"God inhabits the praises of His people!"

Not Just Clowning Around

Sue Neander, California, CMA No. 73,421

What makes you tick? What excites you? For me, it's following the Great Commission to go out and share the gospel by whatever means possible. Often it has been by contributing to missions, especially RFS, knowing that it goes to Open Doors, The JESUS Film Project, and Missionary Ventures International. It's even more exciting to have taught children's groups about Brother Andrew and to have purchased the *JESUS* film in other languages and taken them with me on mission trips for the sole purpose of sharing them with a Christian worker in some other country.

Here at home, my joy has been clowning for the Lord. As "Precious, the Clown," who first ministered with CMA Delta Ambassadors back in the early 90s, it was Matthew 18:5 where Jesus said, *And whoever welcomes a little child like this in my name welcomes me.* I can never read that verse in public without crying. Heaven knows I have tried, but I just can't get through it, because it is absolutely too much to take in–that we, just plain old us, could be welcoming Christ in the flesh! Yet, that is the verse that motivates me to go anywhere and everywhere for Christ.

In August of 2005, I had the awesome opportunity to go on an RFS mission trip to Ecuador with the most wonderful group of CMAers from all over the U.S., and even a couple from Canada, eh? Not only was our team a blessing from day one, so was the missionary family with whom we ministered. Satan really had a job trying to attack us. Since we were so well bonded in ministry, he couldn't use the usual dividing tactics, so he went for sickness to try to wear us down. But this is where maturity and wisdom came in. When our warriors began to fall, the other members of the team just picked up where they left off and continued on. No one outside of our group even knew the difference.

128

During our week in the Andes Mountains a few hours south of Quito, we walked door-to-door in several small towns to invite children and adults to our outreaches in Rio Verde. Some of our members prepared the hall where the evening adult rally was to take place. They did everything from sweeping up the huge dead beetles on the floor and hooking up the sound equipment, to setting up the chairs and rehearsing the vocal portion of the program—all the while praying that people would come. Meanwhile, the children's ministry team held afternoon rallies at the church. We had jump roping outside and a "beauty shop" inside. Every little girl had her hair done in a ponytail or pigtails, and was given colorful clips for decoration. It was a joy to see the little girls come to the evening rally with their parents and still have their hair fancy from the afternoon, but the far greater joy was to pray with adults who came forward following the adult evangelical outreach.

This was no ordinary trip. Not only did we do the usual "mission trip" activities, but we were blessed by Don Wolfram, whose parents had been missionaries there in Ecuador decades ago. He took us to Shell, a town that was the base camp for the martyred missionaries made famous in *Through Gates of Splendor* and *End of the Spear*. But unlike a regular tour guide, Don told us about his parents' ministry colleagues. It was personal for him, and as a result, for us too.

I was thankful to spend a week with such wonderful Christians truly answering the call of our Lord to "Go ye into all the world."

Seek Him Like a Little Child

Russ Williams, Massachusetts, CMA No. 97,419

My first RFS experience touched my heart. On our RFS ride, we stopped in many public places and, in a large group circle, prayed for the upcoming season, the community, the area churches, and each other that God would direct our steps. It was in the middle of one of our prayer circles a little four-year-old boy came out of nowhere looking at all the motorcycles with great excitement. His name was Zachary and he was with his grandmother.

We continued to talk with them and found out that little Zachary had lost his dad recently in a motorcycle race in New Hampshire. Zachary didn't understand why his dad didn't come home. He really did not understand death, so every time he saw motorcycles he was searching for his dad. His love for his dad and passion for motorcycles at such a young age touched me. We should seek our Heavenly Father with the same passion this four-year-old had.

We asked if we could pray for Zachary and his family. The reply was yes, so we put Zach on a bike and prayed for him, his grandmother, and for the family that God would guide their steps and protect them, and most important, that they would find salvation. We gave Zach a copy of the CMA New Testament. When Zach saw the picture of the motorcycle on the cover he held it tight with both hands and we told him to have his grandmother read it to him every night. We also sent pictures to his grandmother and gave her information on who we were and what we were about.

This one RFS was a divine appointment set up by GOD Himself. I was blessed to have witnessed it and as we all continue to pray for Zach I am sure God's Kingdom will be increased and many more will be blessed also.

Please pray for Zach and his family. God has plans for him.

SECTION SIX:

Conclusion

Epilogue

As you have just read about what God is doing both in the United States and around the world, you can see that RFS *is* an extension of the ministry of CMA into the world. Funds from this event reach coast to coast within the United States and around the globe, often working in the background of projects to bring life-changing results. Together, with your help, we are raising up leaders who are training the chapters and members, equipping them for ministry, touching the Kingdom of God. We are providing ministry materials to witness to unbelievers and establishing a follow-up process to show them their place in the family of God. We are pouring love and appreciation into pastors around the world. We are touching those who are persecuted—both at home and abroad. Most of all, we are showing the love of Christ to a world in desperate need of everlasting hope.

You are an important part of making all of this happen. Your involvement, no matter how small it may appear in your eyes, is helping to change the nations—each prayer prayed, each dollar donated, each tear shed moves more mountains than we will ever know, for God's ways are higher than our ways. Know that you are appreciated for all you do.

For more information about the Christian Motorcyclists Association, contact us at:

www.cmausa.org

or

PO Box 9
Hatfield, AR 71945